'A2' ICT

3rd Edition

P.M.Heathcote B.Sc.(Hons), M.Sc.

Published by
Payne-Gallway is an imprint of
Person Education Limited,
a company incorporated in England & Wales,
having its registered office at
Edinburgh Gate, Harlow, Essex, CM20 2JE.
Registered company number: 872828
E-mail: info@payne-gallway.co.uk
Web site: www.payne-gallway.co.uk

Acknowledgements

I would like to thank the many colleagues and friends who have contributed to this book, and I am grateful to the following Examination Boards for permission to use questions from past examination papers:

The Assessment and Qualifications Alliance (AQA), Edexcel Foundation, Northern Ireland Council for the Curriculum, Examinations and Assessment (NICCEA), Scottish Qualifications Authority (SQA), Welsh Joint Education Committee (WJEC).

The answers in the text and in the teacher's supplement are the sole responsibility of the author and have neither been provided nor approved by the examination boards.

I would also like to thank the following organisations for permission to reproduce copyright material in the form of articles, photographs and artwork:

Bradford & Bingley Building Society (Fig 43.3) *Polartechnics Limited*

British Software Alliance (Figures 47.1, 47.3) *Sagesoft Limited (Figure 54.1)*

Formic Limited *The Economist, London*

Machinery *The Guardian*

Network Associates (Figure 48.1) *Times Newspapers Limited*

Graphics editor and designer: Flora Heathcote
Cover picture © "Silence" reproduced with the kind permission of Neil Canning
Cover photography © Mike Kwasniak, 160 Sidegate Lane, Ipswich
Cover design by Tony Burton

First edition 2001 Reprinted 2002
There is no second edition. To avoid confusion, as this is half of 'A' Level ICT 3rd edition, this is the
Third edition 2003, 2005
10 9 8 7 6 5 4

A catalogue entry for this book is available from the British Library.

10-digit ISBN: 1 904467 15 6
13-digit ISBN: 978 1 904467 15 1
Copyright © P.M.Heathcote 2003

Printed in Malta by
Gutenberg Press Limited

Preface

The aim of this book is to provide a comprehensive yet concise textbook covering all the topics studied for the 'A2' modules of the AQA 'A' Level course in Information and Communications Technology.

The book is divided into 2 sections covering all the material for modules 4 and 5 of the specification. Within a section, each chapter covers material that can comfortably be taught in one or two lessons, and the chapters are sequenced in such a way that practical sessions can be based around the theory covered in the classroom.

Sample examination questions and answers are included at the end of each section to show students the type of answers that are likely to score well in the examinations.

Throughout the book, case studies are used to illustrate the points made. Each chapter contains exercises and questions from past examination papers, so that the student can gain plenty of experience in 'exam technique'. Answers to all the questions are available, to teachers only, in a separate Teacher's Supplement which can be downloaded from our web site www.payne-gallway.co.uk

Page numbers have been kept consistent with the full 'A' Level ICT text so that either book can be used as part of a class set.

Contents

Section 4
Information Systems in Organisations   195

Section 5
Information: Policy, Strategy and Systems   287

Appendix A
AQA Specification Summary   350

Table of Contents

SECTION 4

Chapter 36 – Organisational Structure — 196
How organisations work — 196
Ingredients for success — 196
Focus on people — 197
Focus on organisation — 197
External pressures on an organisation — 199
Case study: Preservation vs. the people — 199
Focus on technology — 199
Organisations and information systems — 200
Data processing systems — 200
Knowledge work systems — 201
Management information systems — 201

Chapter 37 – Management Information Systems — 202
Introduction — 202
Information systems vs. data processing systems — 202
Internal and external information — 202
Information flow — 203
The role of a management information system — 203
What managers do — 204
Types of decision — 205
Stages of decision-making — 205
Case study: Buying a new car — 207
Desirable characteristics of a MIS — 207
Factors influencing success or failure of MIS — 207

Chapter 38 – The Information Systems Life Cycle — 210
Overview of the systems life cycle — 210
The waterfall model — 211
What prompts a new system? — 212
Feasibility study — 212
Requirements analysis — 213
Case study: Computer-dating the customer — 213
System design — 214
Implementation — 214
Methods of conversion — 214
Post-implementation review — 215
System maintenance — 215
Prototyping — 216
Benefits of prototyping — 216

Chapter 39 – Implementation of Information Systems — 218
What is implementation? — 218
Successful implementation — 218
Why do information systems fail? — 219
Case study: Tiptree Book Distributors — 220
Factors in successful implementation — 221

Chapter 40 – Information Systems Strategy — 223
Introduction — 223
Formulating an information system strategy — 224
End-user computing — 225
ICT for competitive advantage — 225
Case study: Just-in-time at Wal-Mart's — 226

Chapter 41 – Expert Systems — 228
Definition — 228
Uses of expert systems — 228
Benefits of expert systems in organisations — 228
Limitations of expert systems — 229

Chapter 42 – Information — 230
Sources of information — 230
Levels of information — 230
Quality of information — 230
Case study: Clearing off to College — 231
Channels of communication — 232
Case study: Guides need information — 232
Presenting management information — 232
The intended audience — 233
Graphs and charts — 233
Guidelines for presentations — 234
Keeping everyone informed — 234
Marketing information — 234

Chapter 43 – Data — 236
Data capture — 236
Using bar codes — 236
Other uses of bar codes — 237
Magnetic stripe cards — 237
Linking customers and suppliers through EDI — 237
Smart cards — 238
Case study: A smarter way to pay — 238

Keying in data 238
Case study: Bradford & Bingley 239

Chapter 44 – The Management of Change 241
Outcomes from ICT investments 241
Valuing the workforce 241
Reasons why ICT systems fail 241
Case study: London Ambulance Service 242
Managing change successfully 243
Case study: Pindar 244
Implications of change 245

Chapter 45 – Security Policies 246
Threats to security and integrity 246
Risk analysis 246
Layers of control 247
Building and equipment security 247
Authorisation software 248
Communications security 248
Operational security 248
Audit trail 249
Case study: Harold Shipman, GP and serial killer 249
Personnel safeguards 250
Corporate ICT security policy 250
Case study: War on the Web 251

Chapter 46 – Disaster Recovery 252
Effects of negligence 252
Stages in disaster planning 252
Contents of a security plan 253
Disaster recovery plan 253
Case study: Trust in the Virtual World 253
Criteria used to select a contingency plan 254

Chapter 47 – Implementation of Legislation 255
Laws relating to ICT 255
The Data Protection Act 255
A data protection policy 255
Software copyright 256
Health and Safety 258
Encouraging 'ownership' of workspace 258
Taking regular breaks 259
Providing the right equipment 259
The employer's responsibility 259

Chapter 48 – User Support 260
The need for support 260
The help desk 260
Technical support 260

Help desk software 261
Case study: Call centres 262
Bulletin boards 262
User booklets 263
Newsletters and support articles 263
On-line help 263
Documentation 264

Chapter 49 – Training 265
The need for training 265
Training in the use of information technology 265
Training for senior managers 265
Training for middle managers 265
Training for users 266
Methods of training 266
Computer-based training 266
Instructor-led courses 267
Skills updating 267
Corporate training strategy 267

Chapter 50 – Project Management 269
Introduction 269
Selection of a project manager 269
The tasks of a project manager 269
The project team 269
Project planning and scheduling 270
Project reviews 271
Characteristics of a good team 271

Chapter 51 – Codes of Practice 272
Ethics and computing 272
Factors in ethical decision-making 272
Formal guidelines in the computing industry 272
Codes of practice 274
Employee code of conduct 274
Using informal guidelines to make ethical decisions 274
Case study 1 275
Case study 2 275
Case study 3 275

ICT4 – Sample Questions and Answers 277

SECTION 5

Chapter 52 – Policy and Strategy 286

The challenge of information management 286
Consistency with business priorities 286
Centralisation vs. decentralisation 286
Different user needs 287
Hardware and software choices 288
Emulation software 288
Upgrading hardware and software 289
Future proofing 289
Offers from TIME computer systems:
    Future proof? 290

Chapter 53 – Security and Backup Policies 291

Introduction 291
Backup strategies 291
Full backup 292
Incremental backup 292
Hardware for backups 293
Grandfather-father-son backups 294

Chapter 54 – Software Evaluation 296

Introduction 296
Choosing software 296
Tailoring the software 297
Upgradability 297
Other evaluation criteria 297
Benchmark tests 298
Checking out the manufacturer 298
Evaluation report 298

Chapter 55 – Data Modelling 300

Traditional file approach 300
The database approach 300
The Database Management System
    (DBMS) 301
The conceptual data model 301
Types of relationship 302
Entity-relationship diagrams 302

Chapter 56 – Relational Database Design 304

What is a relational database? 304
Linking database tables 304
Normalisation 305
First normal form 305
Second normal form – Partial key
    dependence test 307
Dealing with a Many-to-Many relationship 307
Third normal form – Non-key dependence
    test 308
Comparing a flat-file system with a
    relational database 308

Chapter 57 – Database Management 310

Database Administration (DBA) 310
The data dictionary 310
The Database Management System
    (DBMS) 311
Querying the database 311
Using SQL 312
Client-server database 312

Chapter 58 – Communication and Information Systems 314

Centralised processing systems 314
Dispersed systems 314
Local area networks (LANs) 315
Client-server and peer-to-peer networks 315
Wide area networks (WANs) 316
Distributed processing 316
Case study: Pubs get a new round of touch
    tills 316
Distributed databases 317
Advantages and limitations of distributed
    databases 318
Using telecommunications for competitive
    advantage 318
Case study: United Parcel Service (UPS) 319
The Internet and the World Wide Web 320
The role of servers and routers 321

Chapter 59 – Network Security and Accounting 323

Introduction 323
Training users about security 323
Access privileges 323
Access control 323
Firewalls 324
Audit controls 324
Performance management 324
Data encryption 325
Accounting software 326

Chapter 60 – Data Communications and Standards 327

Communications software 327
Speed of transmission 327
Modems 327
Serial and parallel transmission 328
Telecommunications standards and
    protocols 328
The development of de facto standards 329
Case study: Microsoft's MS-DOS 329
Internet protocol 329
Addressing mechanisms on the World Wide
    Web 330

Chapter 61 – Human-Computer Interaction 332

Computers in the workplace 332
Psychological factors 332
Short-term memory 333
Long-term memory 333
Designing good software 334
Text versus graphics 334

Chapter 62 – Software Acquisition and Testing 336

Make or buy? 336
End-user-written software 336
Writing software in-house 336
External consultants 337
Buying a package 337
Leasing software 337
Modifying existing packages 337
Criteria for selecting a software solution 338
Software testing 338
Alpha testing 339
Beta testing 339
Failure of software testing 339
Software maintenance 340
Maintenance releases 340

ICT5 – Sample Questions and Answers 342

Appendix A
AQA Specification 350

Index 358

Section 4

Information Systems in Organisations

In this section:

Chapter 36 – Organisational Structure

Chapter 37 – Management Information Systems

Chapter 38 – The Information Systems Life Cycle

Chapter 39 – Implementation of Information Systems

Chapter 40 – Information Systems Strategy

Chapter 41 – Expert Systems

Chapter 42 – Information

Chapter 43 – Data

Chapter 44 – The Management of Change

Chapter 45 – Security Policies

Chapter 46 – Disaster Recovery

Chapter 47 – Implementation of Legislation

Chapter 48 – User Support

Chapter 49 – Training

Chapter 50 – Project Management

Chapter 51 – Codes of Practice

Sample Questions and Answers

Chapter 36 – Organisational Structure

How organisations work

Organisations are entities comprising a range of human and technological resources which are managed, organised and coordinated to accomplish goals. The goal of a business organisation is usually to generate a profit; other types of organisation may have quite different objectives such as the preservation of the environment, military conquest or gaining religious converts.

> ➢ **Discussion: What are the goals of the following organisations? A College of Further Education, a hospital, the BBC, McDonald's, Greenpeace?**

The three fundamental resources of any organisation are

- People;
- Organisation;
- Technology.

The success of an organisation is determined by how well it manages and controls these three resources (the 'pillars' of an organisation), the components of which include the following:

People	*Organisation*	*Technology*
Career	Strategy	Hardware
Education	Policy	Software
Training	Mission Statement	Telecommunications
Employee Attitudes	Culture	Information Systems
Employee Participation	Management	
Employee Monitoring	Bureaucracy	
Work Environment	Competition	
	Environment	

Figure 36.1: The three pillars of an organisation

Ingredients for success

A survey commissioned by the Department of Trade and Industry in 1997 came to the following conclusions about the most successful UK companies.

Winning UK companies:

- Are led by visionary, enthusiastic champions of change;
- Unlock the potential of their people
  - Creating a culture in which employees are genuinely empowered and focused on the customer;

- Investing in people through good communications, teamwork and training;
- Flattening and inverting the organisational pyramid;

- Know their customers
  - Constantly learning from others;
  - Welcoming the challenge of demanding customers to drive innovation and competitiveness;

- Constantly introduce new, differentiated products and services
  - By deep knowledge of their competitors;
  - Encouraging innovation to successfully exploit new ideas;
  - Focusing on core businesses complemented by strategic alliances;

- Exceed their customers' expectations with new products and services.

Nine out of ten of the winning UK companies studied exhibited these characteristics of innovation best practice.

Source: DTI 'Winning' Report 1997

Focus on people

Successful companies view people as a key resource rather than simply as a cost - the competition may copy the product but it cannot copy the people. One of the main tasks of management, therefore, is to enable each person in an organisation to fulfil his or her full potential.

As one MD puts it, "motivated staff will be ten times more productive than unmotivated staff". There is a clear recognition that it is employees who most often meet with the company's customers and that "when customers meet an employee they meet the whole organisation and often judge the whole on that basis".

Training is seen as a key component in achieving empowerment of the individual and in maintaining focus on the customer in order to remain competitive. Not only is training "the epicentre of empowerment", with as much as 100% of employees' time spent on it, but successful companies "use education as a competitive weapon".

Focus on organisation

Business organisations have four internal functions which they must manage and control:

- The **Production** group produces the goods or services;
- The **Sales and Marketing** group sells the product;
- The **Personnel** or **Human Resources** group hires and trains workers;
- The **Finance and Accounting** group seeks funds to pay for all these activities and keeps track of the accounts.

Traditionally, an organisation is structured in a pyramid fashion, as in Figure 36.2.

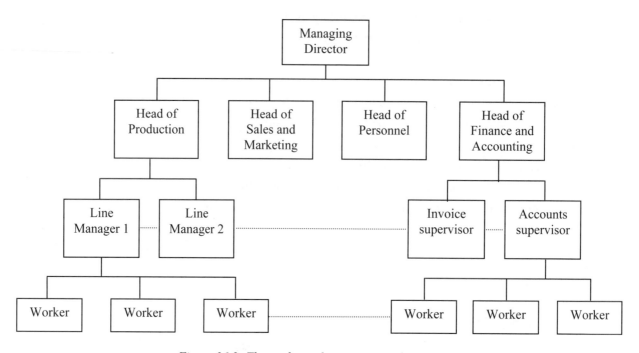

Figure 36.2: The traditional organisational structure

In the late 1990s, changes in working practices resulted in 'flatter' organisations, with layers of middle management disappearing in an effort to eliminate the stifling effects of hierarchy and bureaucracy. As the DTI 'Winning' report says:

"Five years ago the corporate structure was like a pyramid with very steep sides, in fact one could say a stalactite. Now it is more like a plate of peas. The number of levels in an organisation is cut to as few as possible. In some instances there are only three levels within the organisation: Directors, Managers and People".

Turning the organisational pyramid upside down emphasises that customers, markets and competition are crucial to business success, and employees are in the front line, being the major point of contact between the organisation and the customers.

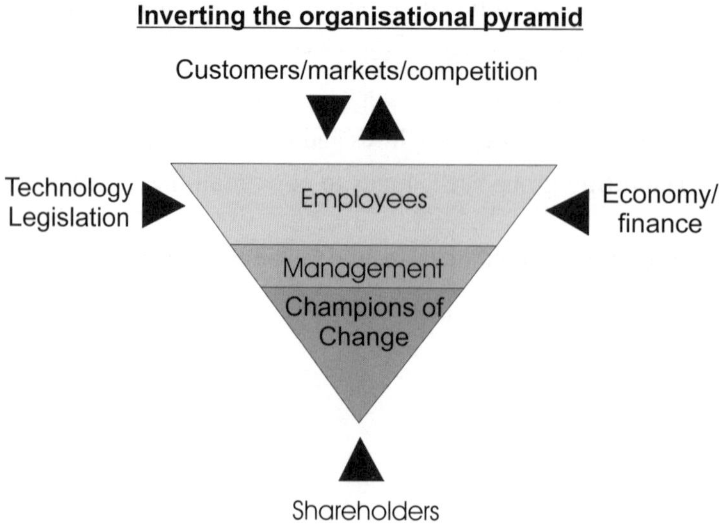

Inverting the organisational pyramid

Customers/markets/competition

Technology Legislation

Employees

Economy/ finance

Management

Champions of Change

Source: DTI 'Winning' Report 1997

Shareholders

Figure 36.3: A different view of organisational structure

External pressures on an organisation

Surrounding the organisation is an environment of customers, competitors, government regulators, pressure groups and other interested parties, all of which have an influence on how the business is run and what policy decisions are made. (See Figure 36.4.)

Figure 36.4: The activities of a business organisation

Case study: Preservation vs. the people

In November 1997 the Guardian carried an article describing the four-year battle over local authority plans to replace the chairlift serving the ski centre of Aviemore with a funicular railway. Conservationists compare it with driving a motorway through Stonehenge while local people say it will bring much-needed jobs and money to the area. The RSPB together with the World Wide Fund for Nature (WWF) have fought the plan to develop a glen that offers one of the most breathtaking views in Scotland, home to the rare black grouse and scene of Landseer's famous tribute to the stag, "Monarch of the Glen". For the people of Strathspey, the funicular railway holds the key to their economic future, and the Government is prepared to contribute £9 million to the £17 million scheme.

➤ **Discussion: This is a good illustration of the external pressures that can be brought to bear on the decision-making process within an organisation. Anyone with an interest in a business is called a "stakeholder". Who are the stakeholders in this case?**

Focus on technology

In the first year of this course you learned about various computer technologies. In this module, you'll learn how technology can be used in building and using information systems in organisations. Technology is the third 'pillar' of a successful organisation.

Organisations and information systems

Most organisations are hierarchical; they are arranged in ascending order of power, pay and privilege. The three major levels in an organisation are production workers (the **operational** level), information workers (the **tactical** level) and management workers (the **strategic** level).

Each level in an organisation has its unique class of information system:

- Data or transaction processing systems serve the needs of production workers who must deal with thousands, or even millions, of transactions with customers and suppliers.

- Knowledge work systems serve the needs of clerical and professional people to process and create information and knowledge.

- Management information systems serve management's needs to control and plan the organisation.

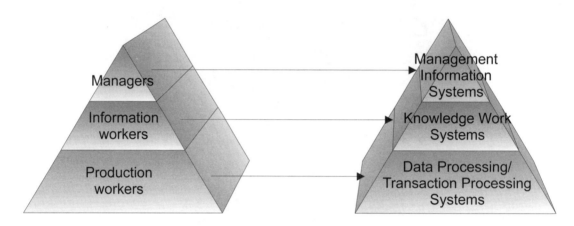

Figure 36.5: Organisations and Information Systems

Organisations, then, do not have just one information system; they may have hundreds. Each of the basic types of systems is described below.

Data processing systems

A data processing system is also known as a **transaction processing system**. Every time you buy an item in a supermarket, withdraw some cash from your bank account, make a hospital appointment or sign up for a college course, a **transaction** has occurred. Transactions are all the events that are recorded when goods or services are bought, sold, distributed or dealt with in some manner.

There are two kinds of transaction processing system:

- Batch systems, whereby transactions are collected over a period of time (say a day or a week) and processed together;

- On-line systems where the data is processed as soon as it is collected.

When there is no immediate urgency for a response or up-to-the-minute information, a batch processing system is often suitable. The TV Licensing Authority, for example, may collect requests for TV licences and process them in batches of 50 or 100 at a time. An airline reservation system, on the other hand, requires up-to-date information on what seats are available, so an on-line system must be used. Such a system is also known as a 'pseudo real-time' system. The word 'pseudo' indicates that processing takes place effectively but not absolutely immediately: a delay of a couple of minutes is normally acceptable.

> **Discussion: What type of transaction processing (batch or on-line) would be suitable for the following?**
> **A mail-order company taking orders by telephone or mail;**
> **A credit-card company processing sales transactions;**
> **A bookshop using electronic point-of-sale tills to keep track of sales and stock;**
> **A hospital appointment system.**

Knowledge work systems

'Information workers' are of two general types: office clerical workers and sales personnel, and behind-the-scenes professionals such as accountants, lawyers, doctors and engineers.

Knowledge work systems are used by information workers to help deal with problems requiring knowledge or technical expertise. Word processing programs, spreadsheets, databases, computer-aided design packages and project management software all fall into this category. In addition, software and hardware that enables groups of people to find out information, communicate or work together as a team, even though they are geographically separated, is of vital importance in large organisations. Networks, web browsers, e-mail facilities and the use of video conferencing are examples of such technology.

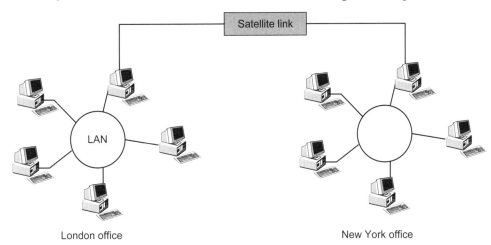

Figure 36.6: Global communications network

Management information systems

Management information systems are designed to help managers monitor and control organisational performance and plan for the future. This type of information system is discussed in more detail in the next chapter.

Exercises

1. Typically, information is communicated at three levels within an organisation. Identify these levels.

(3)

New question

2. An organisation generally consists of different levels, employing production workers, knowledge workers and management.

Give an example of each of these types of worker in a named organisation. (4)

New question

Chapter 37 – Management Information Systems

Introduction

Over the past two decades, a transformation to an information society has been taking place, and computers and telecommunications technologies have revolutionised the way that organisations operate. We live in an information age, and no business of any size can survive and compete without embracing information technology. Information has come to be recognised as a resource of fundamental importance to an organisation, in the same way as the more traditional resources of people, materials and finance.

It is not enough to be merely 'computer-literate' in order to become an expert in information systems. It is also necessary to understand how to apply modern technology in a business, commercial or other environment to achieve the goals of the organisation.

Information systems vs. data processing systems

In the last chapter we looked at the different levels of information system in an organisation.

Remember that a data processing system is simply one which records the day-to-day transactions taking place within an organisation. An information system is one which uses this data and turns it into useful information. For example:

- Data on items sold is collected by the **data processing system**, using a barcode scanner and an EPOS system, and stored on a computer file;

- An **operational information system** then reads this data and produces a list of items that need reordering;

- A **management information system** may analyse the sales data to highlight sales trends and use this information to plan a new marketing campaign, adjust price levels or plan an increase or reduction in production facilities.

Internal and external information

Much of the information used by management concerns the **internal** operations of the company. However, **external** information about the environment in which the organisation exists is crucial to all organisations. This may include

- Intelligence gathering about competitors' activities;

- Information about population shifts;

- Economic and social factors;

- Government legislation.

This type of information is of great importance to managers who are trying to shave production costs, find new markets, develop new products, or have strategic decisions to make about the future direction of the company. Information is collected in many ways – through conversations and interpersonal 'networking', reading newspapers, trade reviews and magazines, attending conferences and meetings, browsing the Internet. A **formal information system** relies on procedures for the collecting, storing, processing and accessing of data in order to obtain information.

> ➢ An international car manufacturing company maintains a database holding details of every car that will be made over the next ten years by every other car manufacturer in the world. This data is collected through agencies specialising in information gathering, through trade fairs and reviews, 'leaks' and even industrial espionage.
>
> A special department exists to collect and collate this information. One of the manager's jobs is to read every relevant magazine, newspaper article and communication every morning, highlight anything of importance and pass the pile of paper round the department for the others to read prior to the database being updated.

Information flow

Information flows through an organisation through both formal and informal information systems. Informal ways of gathering information include face-to-face conversations, meetings, telephone conversations, reading newspapers and magazines, listening to radio and television and surfing the Internet.

Information is also circulated through company newsletters, memos and notice boards. The problem with newsletters and memos is that readers often have so much information to absorb that they quickly forget it.

Formal methods of disseminating information around an organisation include the following:

- Computerised information systems which allow users to query databases over a company-wide network. Internal data is often collected in the first instance through transaction processing systems. External data can be collected, for example, through agencies such as Dun and Bradstreet which produces an on-line electronic data service called 'DataStream' to both business and academic organisations.

- Software packages such as Lotus Notes enable people at different locations to have the same document on their screens and work on it together. Appointments can be held on the systems so that meetings can be arranged at a time when everyone is free.

- E-mail allows correspondence and files to be transmitted throughout an organisation as well as to others outside the organisation.

- Company-wide Intranets are networks which work on the same principle as the Internet but are for use within the organisation. Information can be disseminated throughout an organisation via the Intranet rather than in the form of written memos and newsletters.

The role of a management information system

The role of a management information system is to convert data from internal and external sources into information that can be used to aid in making effective decisions for planning, directing and controlling the activities for which they are responsible. An organisation may have dozens of different information systems, some of which are useful for the day-to-day operational decisions, and some of which are used in making tactical and strategic decisions.

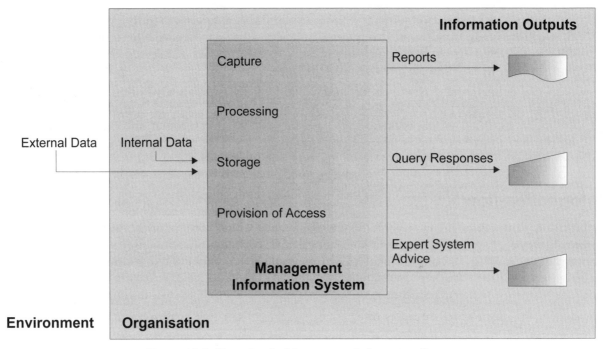

Figure 37.1: The role of a Management Information System

What managers do

To understand how information systems can benefit managers, we first need to examine what the functions of management are and the kind of information they need for decision-making.

The five classical functions of managers (described more than 70 years ago) are:

1. **Planning.** Managers plan the direction a company is to take, whether to diversify, which areas of the world to operate in, how to maximise profit.

2. **Organising**. Resources such as people, space, equipment and services must be organised.

3. **Coordinating**. Managers coordinate the activities of various departments.

4. **Decision-making**. Managers make decisions about the organisation, the products or services made or sold, the employees, the use of information technology.

5. **Controlling**. This involves monitoring and supervising the activities of others.

Management information systems must be designed to support managers in as many of these functions as possible, at different levels (operational, tactical, strategic) of an organisation.

> ➢ **Discussion: How could a MIS help college managers at various levels to carry out activities of planning, organising, coordinating, decision-making and controlling?**

A study in 1973 by Henry Mintzberg found that managers divided up their time as shown in the pie chart below. He described the work of a manager as consisting of hundreds of brief activities of great variety, requiring rapid shifts of attention from one issue to another, very often initiated by emerging problems. Half of the activities of chief executives lasted less than 9 minutes.

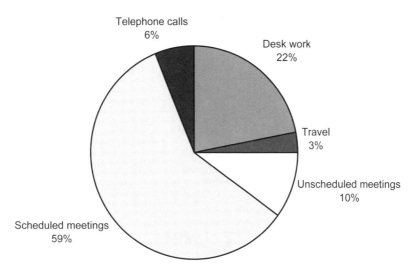

Figure 37.2: How managers spent their time in 1973

> ➤ **Discussion: Today's managers still spend their time divided between many activities. Do you think there are any activities which managers spend more time on than they did in 1973?**

Types of decision

Management decisions can be classified into two types – *structured* and *unstructured*. Structured decisions are repetitive, routine and involve a definite procedure for handling them. Unstructured decisions on the other hand are decisions which require judgement, insight and evaluation. They are often important decisions and there is no set procedure for making them.

> ➤ **Discussion: Categorise the following decisions to be made by a department store manager as structured or unstructured:**
>
>   **In which town shall we open the next branch?**
>
>   **How many extra staff shall we hire to cope with the Christmas rush?**
>
>   **What shall we do about an employee who has had 30 sick days in the last 6 months?**
>
>   **Should we try and increase the number of customers who hold a store card?**

Stages of decision-making

Making unstructured, non-routine decisions is a process that takes place over a period of time, and consists of several stages. Think of any important decision that you may have to make, like whether to go on to University or get a job, which college or University to attend, what course or career to follow. You will probably reach any of these decisions over a period of time, having gathered together information from various sources and listened to friends, parents or careers advisers.

The manager who has non-routine decisions to make typically goes through the following stages:

1. **Recognition that there is a problem.** An information system is useful at this stage to keep managers informed of how well the department or organisation is performing and to let them know where problems exist. The principle of exception reporting is especially important in this stage – in other

words, only situations which need some action are reported. (For example, customers with outstanding accounts, a sudden drop or increase in sales compared with the same period last year or a rash of staff resignations.)

2. **Consideration of possible solutions.** More detailed information may be needed at this stage, or possibly tools such as a spreadsheet which can model the effect of different solutions such as price increases or decreases, staff pay increases etc.

3. **Choosing a solution.**

4. **Implementing the solution**. This may involve setting up a new management information system to report on the progress of the solution.

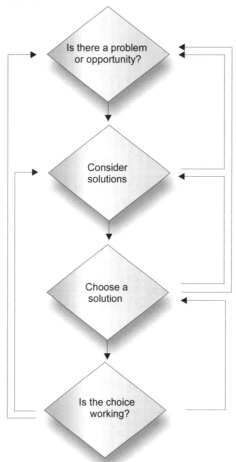

Figure 37.3: The decision-making process

Most decisions do not proceed smoothly from one stage to the next, and backtracking to a previous stage is often required if a chosen solution turns out to be impossible or new information comes to light which offers alternative choices.

Making structured decisions – often of an operational nature – is made easier by having an information system which provides the information necessary to make the correct decisions.

> ➢ **Discussion: A car company gathers information about its customer base through many sources, including market research surveys. One company has discovered that it has relatively few customers in the 18-30 age range. How can this information be used by the company to improve its sales?**

Case study: Buying a new car

If you want to purchase a new car from a Ford dealer, chances are that the make and model you want, in the right colour with the right accessories, is not in stock. It's just too expensive to have cars with every possible combination of options sitting in the parking lot waiting for a customer. In the past, it's been almost impossible for dealers to track down exactly the model that a customer wants.

With the new information system, the dealer can type the details of the required car into a terminal connected to the main Ford plant at Dagenham. The information will then come back to tell the dealer whether there are any cars available of that specification, and exactly where they are. They may be on the Ford parking lot, or there may be only two available, one at a dealer's in Perth and the other in Bournemouth. There may be none available – in which case Ford will make one for you, though this may take some time.

Plant production managers are also connected to the system, and so they know exactly what cars have been ordered and can adjust production to reflect demand every day.

➤ **Discussion: This is an example of a management information system. How does it help**

  – **the dealer?**

  – **the customer?**

  – **the manufacturer?**

Desirable characteristics of a MIS

Formal information systems are useful at every level of an organisation. Operational systems provide answers to specific, routine questions on screen or through regular daily, weekly or monthly reports. A senior manager is likely to need information which comes to light from a new way of analysing the available data, or information from external sources.

Systems designers need to try to design management information systems which have the following characteristics:

- They are flexible, allowing for many different ways of analysing data and evaluating information;

- They are capable of supporting a range of skills and knowledge;

- They help managers get things done through interpersonal communication with other members of the organisation;

- Because managers are busy people who switch rapidly between different tasks, they should not require extensive periods of concentration;

- They should make it easy to interrupt the work and return to it at a later time;

- They should protect a manager, as far as possible, from information overload.

Factors influencing success or failure of MIS

Management information systems are generally enormously complex, and their selection, design and implementation will involve dozens of people from both within and outside the organisation. The managers and directors who are ultimately responsible for ensuring the success of the system need to have not only an intimate knowledge and appreciation of exactly what they want out of the system. They must be aware of the possibilities that ICT systems can offer, the difficulties that may be encountered and the importance of having in place the proper procedures to ensure the smooth functioning of the system.

Failure of management information systems can attributed to a number of reasons such as:

- **Inadequate analysis.** The potential problems, exact needs and constraints are not fully understood before the design or selection of a new system;

- **Lack of management involvement in design.** It is essential that all those expecting and needing to benefit from a new system are involved in its design. Without this involvement, any system is doomed to failure either by providing information which nobody needs (or, worse still, nobody understands) or management having expectations from a new system which cannot be delivered.

- **Emphasis on the computer system.** Selecting the right hardware and software is clearly essential as the basis for a modern computer system but appropriate procedures for handling both data input and output must be established before a system is implemented. The objectives of the new system need to be clearly thought out. Users often request the population of fields on a database for no explained reason and often request management reports which are neither useful nor read!

- **Concentration on low-level data processing.** One of the fundamental functions of a system within a company is the day-to-day processing of transactions, including sales and purchase orders, invoices, goods receipts and credit notes. When designing a basic system, the management information available from the system must be both easily accessible and easily understandable by users who may be neither computer literate nor managers.

- **Lack of management knowledge of ICT systems and their capabilities.** Managers require information for running companies or departments, and among other things, for producing budgets and forecasts. Managers must know what they want from a system but it cannot be assumed that these same managers have a full (or even a slight) grasp of the technology which will provide the information they need.

- **Lack of teamwork.** The needs of the accounts department, the marketing department, the sales department (home and export), and the storage and despatch departments are all likely to differ and an ICT manager needs not only to lead his team but also to be able to take on board the whole company's requirements. Teamwork needs leadership and a good leader is one who can convince all the members of a company team that the ICT system being designed is going to meet everybody's needs – but not necessarily in quite the way that the different players may have pictured.

- **Lack of professional standards.** Clear documentation written in a language that not only the ICT manager can understand is essential for training, implementation and daily use of a new system. Operators need to know exactly what to do in their work (including what to do if they need to undo some action); managers need to feel reassured that, if necessary, explanations are available to help them to interrogate the system for the information they require, and all people using the system must feel confident enough to be able to help others.

(Thanks to John Walsh of BEBC for contributing these thoughts after the installation of their new computer system – which, I hasten to add, is a complete success!)

Exercises

1. (a) What is the purpose of a Management Information System?   (1)

    (b) Why is such a system required by managers of an organisation?   (1)

    (c) Give **one** example of the use of a Management Information System within an organisation, clearly stating its purpose.   (2)

    NEAB IT04 Qu 1 1997

2. List **three** desirable features of a management information system, stating in each case why the feature you have specified is useful.   (6)

    New question

3. A school is planning the introduction of a computer-based attendance system for classes and registration groups. The purpose of the system is to produce information for the following end-users:

    - Class teachers

    - Tutors/Head of Year

    - Senior managers (e.g. Deputy Head)

    (a) Describe **three** alternative ways of collecting the information for the system.   (6)

    (b) For each of the different end-users describe, with the aid of an example, information that the system might produce in relation to their requirements.   (6)

    NEAB IT04 Qu 3 1997

4. With the aid of appropriate examples, explain the difference between formal and informal information flows.   (6)

    NEAB IT04 Qu 2 1998

5. A company keeps records of its sales and uses a Management Information System to produce reports for its sales personnel and for its shareholders.

    (a) Describe two differences between the information needed by sales personnel in their day-to-day work, and by shareholders reading the annual report.   (4)

    (b) Describe, with the aid of an example, one characteristic of good quality information that might be produced by this system.   (3)

    AQA ICT4 Qu 6 June 2002

6. Company management sometimes introduce new information and communication systems, giving little advance notice to their staff. This may contribute to the failure of these systems, and cause other problems for their staff.

    (a) State **six** factors that may cause the failure of a system that has been introduced too quickly. (6)

    (b) Describe three problems that staff might encounter in this situation.   (6)

    AQA ICT4 Qu 3 January 2003

Chapter 38 – The Information Systems Life Cycle

Overview of the systems life cycle

Large systems development projects may involve dozens of people working over several months or even years, so they cannot be allowed to proceed in a haphazard fashion. The goals of an information system must be thoroughly understood, and formal procedures and methods applied to ensure that the project is delivered on time and to the required specification.

The systems life cycle methodology approaches the development of information systems in a very methodical and sequential manner. Each stage is composed of certain well-defined activities and responsibilities, and is completed before the next stage begins. This approach was popular in the 1960s and 70s, when systems were largely transaction-processing systems and had a much heavier reliance on programming than most modern information systems, which are database-oriented.

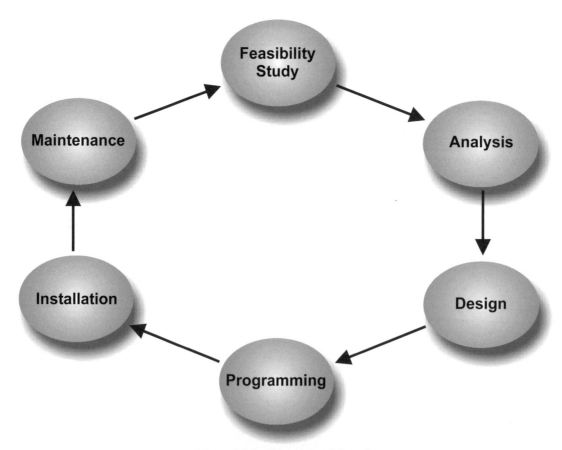

Figure 38.1: The systems life cycle

> ➢ **Discussion: In your experience of practical work on information technology projects, is this a good representation of the process of implementing a system from scratch? If not, why not?**

The waterfall model

The systems life cycle approach to development is also known as the 'waterfall model', and a variation on the basic diagram of 38.1 is shown in Figure 38.2.

Note that the arrows go up and down the 'waterfall', reflecting the fact that developers often have to rework earlier stages in the light of experience gained as development progresses.

A project milestone terminates each stage of a life-cycle-oriented approach. At this stage, the 'deliverable' resulting from that stage – such as the documentation for the analysis or the design, or the program code or finished database application, is *signed off* by all concerned parties and approval is given to proceed. The 'concerned parties' usually include the end-users, the management and the developers, as well as other experts such as database administration personnel. This sequence continues until the evaluation stage has been completed and the finished system is delivered to the end-users.

In this model, the end-user has very little say in the development process, which is carried out by technical specialists such as systems analysts and programmers. He or she is presented with the finished system at the end of the development cycle and if it is not quite what was wanted, it is generally too late to make changes. Therefore, it is extremely important that the system requirements are very clearly specified and understood by all parties before being signed off.

Such levels of certainty are difficult to achieve and this is one of the major drawbacks of the 'waterfall model'.

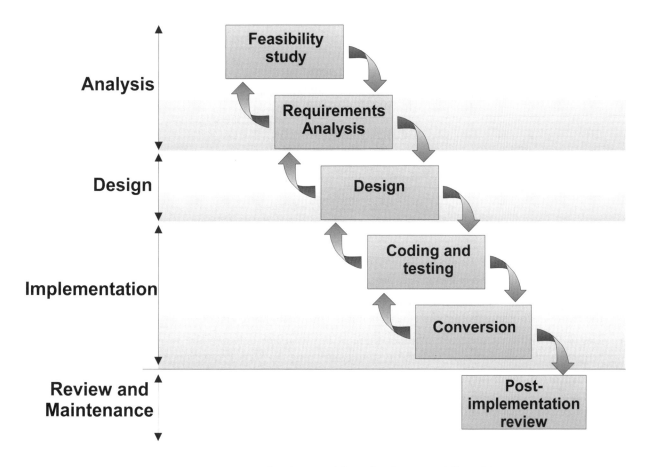

Figure 38.2: Systems development life cycle (the 'Waterfall model')

What prompts a new system?

The development of a new information system is a major undertaking and not one to be undertaken lightly. Wal-Mart, an American discount store, spent $700m on its new computerised distribution system in the 1980s. Tesco, Sainsbury's and Marks and Spencer have spent massive sums of money on their computer systems in the past decade. Businesses must adapt to remain competitive. Some of the reasons for introducing a new system may be:

1. **The current system may no longer be suitable for its purpose**. Changes in work processes, expansion of the business, changes in business requirements or the environment in which the organisation operates may all lead to a reassessment of information system requirements.

2. **Technological developments may have made the current system redundant or outdated**. Advances in hardware, software and telecommunications bring new opportunities which an organisation cannot ignore if it is to keep ahead of its rivals.

3. **The current system may be too inflexible or expensive to maintain**, or may reduce the organisation's ability to respond quickly enough to customer's demands.

Feasibility study

This is the first stage of the systems life cycle. The **scope** and **objectives** of the proposed system must be written down. The aim of the feasibility study is to understand the problem and to determine whether it is worth proceeding. There are five main factors to be considered:

Technical feasibility

Economic feasibility

Legal feasibility

Operational feasibility

Schedule feasibility

Figure 38.3: TELOS – a mnemonic for the five feasibility factors

- **Technical feasibility** means investigating whether the technology exists to implement the proposed system, or whether this is a practical proposition.

- **Economic feasibility** has to do with establishing the cost-effectiveness of the proposed system – if the benefits do not outweigh the costs, then it is not worth going ahead.

- **Legal feasibility** determines whether there is any conflict between the proposed system and legal requirements – for example, will the system contravene the Data Protection Act?

- **Operational feasibility** is concerned with whether the current work practices and procedures are adequate to support the new system. It is also concerned with social factors – how the organisational change will affect the working lives of those affected by the system.

- **Schedule feasibility** looks at how long the system will take to develop, or whether it can be done in a desired time-frame.

The completion of this stage is marked by the production of a feasibility report produced by the systems analyst. If the report concludes that the project should go ahead, and this is agreed by senior managers, detailed requirements analysis will proceed.

Requirements analysis

The second phase of systems analysis is a more detailed investigation into the current system and the requirements of the new system.

Gathering details about the current system will involve:

- Interviewing staff at different levels of the organisation from the end-users to senior management.

- Examining current business and systems documents and output. These may include current order documents, computer systems procedures and reports used by operations and senior management.

- Sending out questionnaires and analysing responses. The questions have to be carefully constructed to elicit unambiguous answers.

- Observation of current procedures, by spending time in various departments. A time and motion study can be carried out to see where procedures could be made more efficient, or to detect where bottlenecks occur.

The systems analyst's report will examine how data and information flow around the organisation, and may use **data flow diagrams** to document the flow. It will also establish precisely and in considerable detail exactly what the proposed system will do (as opposed to how it will do it). It will include an in-depth analysis of the costs and benefits, and outline the process of system implementation, including the organisational change required. It must establish who the end-users are, what information they should get and in what form and how it will be obtained.

Alternative options for the implementation of the project will be suggested. These could include suggestions for:

- Whether development should be done in-house or using consultants;

- What hardware configurations could be considered;

- What the software options are.

The report will conclude with a recommendation to either proceed or abandon the project.

Case study: Computer-dating the customer

When it started a century ago, marketing treated all customers the same. By the 1960s, marketers were able to break that anonymous mass into segments. Now customer databases allow them to treat customers as individuals. They may know consumers' names and addresses, what they buy, what they have stopped buying and even how they respond to a rise in the price of dog food.

For big multinational retailers, this is the equivalent of going back to the days of the individual store owner who knew and greeted each customer personally. The benefits are potentially huge: instead of spending millions on advertising beamed at people who may be indifferent or even hostile to it, retailers can use databases to help them hang on to their existing customers and persuade them to buy more. But it is not trouble-free: databases are expensive to collect and analyse, and some customers may see such individual marketing as an invasion of their privacy.

Talbot's, a 385-store women's clothing chain based in Massachusetts, has compiled a database of 7m names that includes information about customers' sizes. This has enabled them to forecast more accurately which sizes will sell in particular stores. It also asks all customers for their post codes when they pay, to help it plan new store openings. The effort seems to be paying off. For the past five years the company has been opening around 50 new stores a year.

Source: The Economist 4 March 1995

> ➤ **Discussion: A system like the one above would have cost millions of dollars to install. What were the major costs? What were the benefits?**

System design

The design specifies the following aspects of a system:

- The hardware platform – which type of computer, network capabilities, input, storage and output devices;
- The software – programming language, package or database;
- The outputs – report layouts and screen designs;
- The inputs – documents, screen layouts and validation procedures;
- The user interface – how users will interact with the computer system;
- The modular design of each program in the application;
- The test plan and test data;
- Conversion plan – how the new system is to be implemented;
- Documentation including systems and operations documentation. Later, a user manual will be produced.

Implementation

This phase includes both the coding and testing of the system, the acquisition of hardware and software and the installation of the new system or conversion of the old system to the new one.

The installation phase can include:

- Installing the new hardware, which may involve extensive recabling and changes in office layouts;
- Training the users on the new system;
- Conversion of master files to the new system, or creation of new master files.

Methods of conversion

There are several different methods of conversion:

- **Direct changeover.** The user stops using the old system one day and starts using the new system the next — usually over a weekend or during a slack period. The advantage of this system is that it is fast and efficient, with minimum duplication of work involved. The disadvantage is that normal operations could be seriously disrupted if the new system has errors in it or does not work quite as expected.
- **Parallel conversion.** The old system continues alongside the new system for a few weeks or months. The advantage is that results from the new system can be checked against known results, and if any difficulties occur, operations can continue under the old system while the errors or omissions are sorted out. The disadvantage of parallel conversion is the duplication of effort required to keep both systems running, which may put a strain on personnel.
- **Phased conversion.** This is used with larger systems that can be broken down into individual modules that can be implemented separately at different times. It could also be used where for example only a few customer accounts are processed using the new system, while the rest remain for a time on the old system. Phased conversion could be direct or parallel.
- **Pilot conversion.** This means that the new system will be used first by only a portion of the organisation, for example at one branch or factory.

> ➢ **Discussion: For each of the following examples, state with reasons what type of conversion method would be suitable.**

(a) **A bakery is introducing a system to input orders from each salesperson and use this data to calculate how much of each product to bake each day, and also to calculate the salesperson's commission.**

(b) **A chain store is introducing EPOS terminals connected to a mainframe computer which holds details of stock levels and prices.**

(c) **A public library is introducing a computerised system for the lending and return of books.**

(d) **A large hospital is introducing a computerised system for keeping patient records and appointments.**

(e) **A College is introducing a computerised timetabling and room allocation system.**

(f) **A Company manufacturing electronic components is introducing an integrated system for production control, stock control and order processing.**

(g) **A Local Authority is introducing a computerised system for the collection of a new type of tax.**

Post-implementation review

An important part of the implementation is a review of how the new system is performing, once it has been up and running for a period of time. Minor programming errors may have to be corrected, clerical procedures amended, or modifications made to the design of reports or screen layouts. Often it is only when people start to use a new system that they realise its shortcomings! In some cases they may realise that it would be possible to get even more useful information from the system than they realised, and more programs may be requested. The process of **system maintenance**, in fact, has already begun, and the life cycle is complete.

System maintenance

All software systems require maintenance, and in fact the vast majority of programmers are employed to maintain existing programs rather than to write new ones. There are differing reasons for this, and different types of maintenance.

- **Perfective maintenance**. This implies that while the system runs satisfactorily, there is still room for improvement. For example, extra management information may be needed so that new report programs have to be written. Database queries may be very slow, and a change in a program may be able to improve response time.

- **Adaptive maintenance**. All systems will need to adapt to changing needs within a company. As a business expands, for example, there may be a requirement to convert a standalone system to a multi-user system. New and better hardware may become available, and changes to the software may be necessary to take advantage of this. New government legislation may mean that different methods of calculating tax, for example, are required. Competition from other firms may mean that systems have to be upgraded in order to maintain a competitive edge.

- **Corrective maintenance**. Problems frequently surface after a system has been in use for a short time, however thoroughly it was tested. Some part of the system may not function as expected, or a report might be wrong in some way; totals missing at the bottom, incorrect sequence of data, wrong headings, etc. Frequently errors will be hard to trace, if for example a file appears to have been wrongly updated.

Prototyping

The waterfall model of the system life cycle has major shortcomings and often bears little relation to what happens in practice. One reason for this is that it doesn't allow for modifications to the design as the project proceeds, with both user and developer learning as they go along. Users frequently have difficulty in explaining their requirements at the start of a proposed system since they do not know what is possible and cannot visualise how the final system will work. This can result in a system which does not really match their requirements. (See Figure 39.2.)

Using the **prototyping** approach, a model of a new system is built in order to evaluate it or have it approved before building the production model. Applied to software projects, this means, for example, using special software to quickly design input screens and create a program to input and validate data. This gives the user a chance to experience the 'look and feel' of the input process and suggest alterations before going any further. The earlier a user is involved, the easier it will be to make changes.

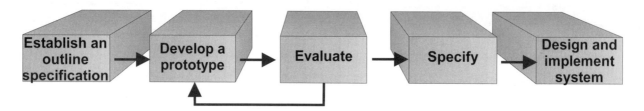

Figure 38.4: The prototyping approach

Benefits of prototyping

The benefits of prototyping are:

- Misunderstandings between software developers and users can be identified when the prototype is demonstrated;

- Missing functions may be detected;

- Incomplete or inconsistent user requirements may be detected and can be completed or corrected;

- A prototype version will be quickly available to demonstrate the feasibility and usefulness of the proposed system to management;

- The prototype can sometimes be used for training before the final system is delivered.

Prototyping may be used in a number of different ways, and various terms have been coined to describe them:

- **Piloting** – using a prototype to test the feasibility of a design proposal;

- **Modelling** – building to develop an understanding of the user's requirements;

- **Throw-away prototyping** – both piloting and modelling are 'throw-away prototypes': once they have achieved their purpose the real system is built;

- **Evolutionary prototyping** – each prototype built represents a step closer to the final solution.

Exercises

1. A feasibility study will often be carried out at an early stage of system development. As well as finding out if the proposal is technically possible the study will also consider economic and social feasibility.

    In the context of a feasibility study describe **one** cost, **one** benefit and **three** possible social effects that would be considered. (5)
    AEB AS Computing Qu 7 1996

2. Often the most critical phase in the systems life cycle is the changeover from the old system to the new one. This may be implemented by *parallel running* or by *pilot running*. Briefly describe these installation methods. (3)
    AEB AS Computing Qu 4 1997

3. State **three** different methods of fact finding available during the systems analysis stage of the systems life cycle, and for **each** of these three methods, give **one** reason for its use. (6)
    AEB Computing Paper 1 Qu 11 1996

4. State and briefly describe **two** different types of program maintenance. (2)
    NEAB Computing Paper 2 Qu 1 1995

5. Describe **five** main stages in the full life cycle of a computerised system. (10)
    NEAB Computing Paper 1 Qu 11 1995

6. Some of the steps in computerising an existing manual system are:
    - systems analysis
    - systems design
    - programming
    - testing
    - changeover to the new system
    - operation and maintenance.

    (a) Describe **three** aspects of the existing manual system which would have to be investigated so that the analysis could be carried out. (3)

    (b) Briefly describe **four** tasks which will be performed during the design process. (4)

    (c) Explain how it is possible for all the individual component modules to pass their tests and yet for the system still to fail. (3)

    (d) The changeover to the new system from the manual system can be achieved in three ways:
    - (i) immediate change;
    - (ii) running the manual and computerised systems in parallel;
    - (iii) gradually introducing the new system a subsystem at a time.

    In **each** case, state an application for which the technique is most appropriate. (3)

    (e) Briefly describe the responsibilities of the systems analyst once the system is operational. (2)
    London Paper 1 Qu 13 1994

Chapter 39 – Implementation of Information Systems

What is implementation?

Implementation is the process of preparing people for the introduction of a new system and actually introducing it. Preparation work can start early in the systems development life cycle, even preceding the development stage. A major new system runs a high risk of failure if its implementation is not very carefully planned and the organisational changes that will be required not fully recognised and allowed for. A fully developed system may be regarded by its developers as a success because it 'works', and yet never become operational, or fall into disuse after a short trial period.

Successful implementation

As part of your course you will probably analyse, design and develop an information system for a real user. This will include scheduling the various stages of implementation, and evaluating its success. You are in fact doing on a small scale what the developers of any system, large or small, have to do. So what are the criteria for judging the success of a system? Here are some possible measures:

- **High level of use**. Is the new system actually used? New systems for recording student results, registering students' presence using swipe cards, or constructing timetables and scheduling classroom use may all be introduced but not be widely accepted. A new customer information system may never become operational because users discover it simply takes too long to enter the data.

- **High level of user satisfaction.** Do users like the system? Large companies may identify products and services provided by the information systems unit (such as e-mail or Intranet services, network services, new software) and ask users to fill in questionnaires to gauge their level of satisfaction with each product or service.

- **Accomplishment of original objectives.** A comprehensive list of objectives should have been stated in the Analysis stage of system development. Have these objectives been satisfactorily achieved? The objectives may be, for example, to perform certain tasks such as recording student grades or sending out invoices in a shorter time than before, to increase market share of a particular product or to produce more accurate estimates of building costs.

- **Appropriate nature of use.** A high level of use is not always an indication that a system is a complete success. Witness the man who called a PC manufacturer to complain that his coffee-mug holder had broken. The puzzled service engineer, on quizzing the customer, finally realised he was referring to the CD drive. Software, too, can be used inappropriately if training is not given.

- **Institutionalisation of the system**. A successful system will be taken on board enthusiastically by users and used in new and changing ways, evolving to meet new demands.

> ➢ **Discussion: Think of some large-scale information systems that have been successfully implemented. What makes these systems so successful?**

Why do information systems fail?

Information systems fail for many reasons at any stage of the systems life cycle.

1. **Analysis**
   - Not enough time and money is spent researching the problem, and objectives are poorly defined, so that benefits will be hard to measure.
   - The project team is not properly staffed, with team members being allocated only when available so that they cannot dedicate themselves to the task, resulting in a lack of continuity and commitment.
   - Users are not sufficiently involved.
   - Analysts have poor communication skills and do not ask the right questions or extract the necessary information to establish what the problems are with the current system or what the requirements of the new system are.

2. **Design**
   - Users have little involvement and the design therefore does not reflect their requirements.
   - The system is designed to meet current needs but is not flexible enough to respond to changes in the business environment.
   - Management is not involved in the design, or makes excessive and inappropriate demands with no real understanding of information technology and its capabilities.
   - Major changes to clerical procedures are planned with no regard to the impact on staffing or the organisation.

3. **Programming**
   - The amount of time required for programming is grossly underestimated.
   - Programmers lack the necessary skills: too much time is spent on coding and not enough on proper program design.
   - Programs are not properly documented and so disruption occurs when any of the team leaves.
   - Not enough resources such as computer time are allocated.

4. **Testing**
   - The project team does not develop a proper test plan.
   - Users are not sufficiently involved in testing. They do not help by creating test data and tests with expected results specified.
   - Acceptance tests are not devised, conducted and signed off by management.

5. **Conversion**
   - Insufficient time and money is allocated for converting the data to the new system.
   - Training is not given to the users, or is only started when the system is installed.
   - User documentation is inadequate.
   - Performance evaluations are not conducted.

With so much to go wrong, it seems quite amazing that so many systems are successfully implemented! The key lies in careful planning and heavy involvement from both users and management combined with technological expertise.

Case study: Tiptree Book Distributors

Tiptree is a book distributor holding books from many different publishers in its huge warehouse and distributing them to bookshops and libraries around the country as orders come in. One of the largest distributors in Britain, it has 10 acres of warehousing and 25 million books in the warehouse, and in 1994 won the British Book Awards Distributor of the Year. It was able to guarantee that any order received would be dispatched by the following day.

Tiptree wanted to ensure that it stayed at the top – and had plans to put in place a computerised warehousing system that would be so much more efficient that all orders would be filled the same day. Under the manual system, when an order was received from a bookshop, warehouse staff would have to travel all over the warehouse finding the correct titles to put in the box. Then to fill the next order they might have to go right to the far end of the warehouse again.

The new computerised system would hold a map of where every book was positioned in the warehouse. The orders would be entered into the computer, which would work out the most efficient way for books to be picked off the shelves and put onto a new conveyor belt system. The system automatically issued an invoice, advising if books were out of stock. The dimensions and weight of each book were entered so that the computer could automatically pick the right sized box to pack the books in, and double-check the consignment was correct by weighing the box before heat-sealing it and dispatching it.

The system worked perfectly during trials. Tests were carried out with every aspect of the hardware, software and warehouse equipment functioning as they would when the system went live. Tiptree's management was so confident of success that they decided to use a 'direct conversion' method of implementation – stop using the old system one day, and start up the new system the next.

Almost immediately, things started to go wrong.

The warehouse staff did not appreciate the need to pick the books off the shelves exactly as instructed by the computer. If the books were awkward to reach, they would take them from a more convenient shelf. This meant that the computer's map showed the correct pallet of books as being out of stock and in need of replenishment, and the incorrectly dispatched pallet as being still on the shelf when in fact it had gone.

After a few weeks, the computer's map became hopelessly inaccurate. The problem was made worse because as the system deteriorated and customers began to complain about books not being delivered, warehouse staff started to circumvent the computer system and take books off the shelf themselves for immediate dispatch. At this point there were no reliable manual stock records for backup, and it also transpired that the map had not been completely accurate in the first place because staff hadn't transferred data from the old manual system to the new computerised system completely accurately.

With the stock records now corrupted, staff were unable to find books to put onto the conveyor belt within the two-hour period allotted by the computer. After this time the books were marked out of stock and the customers did not receive their orders. Meanwhile, some perfectly packed orders were rejected by the computer system because they were underweight. This turned out to be because the programmers had not allowed for the fact that paperback books lose moisture in a warehouse and so weigh a few grams less. Also, some warehouse staff had mistakenly keyed in the dimensions of the box instead of the book, so the computer thought that only one book would fit into a large box. To add to the problem, the computer would allocate a box to be filled with books it thought were in stock but which could not be found anywhere.

One retailer received six pallets of one title, another received three beautifully packed, heat-sealed boxes which contained no books at all. Waterstone's in Croydon opened a large box that should have contained many titles to find inside a single book: *Chaos* by James Gleick.

As the managing director of Tiptree said: "It took 27 years to build up a reputation as the best distributor in the country, and 7 weeks to lose it".

The story has a happy ending – by 1995 the system was yielding the promised rewards and 98% of orders were dispatched the same day as they were received, and the systems have become a model for the book trade.

(Adapted from Tony Collins' account of this implementation in his book 'Crash')

➤ **Discussion: What were the major errors in the implementation of Tiptree's system? Could these have been avoided? Think of at least three things they could have done differently in order to ensure a smooth changeover from the old system to the new one.**

Factors in successful implementation

Some recognised factors in successful system implementation are shown in Figure 39.1.

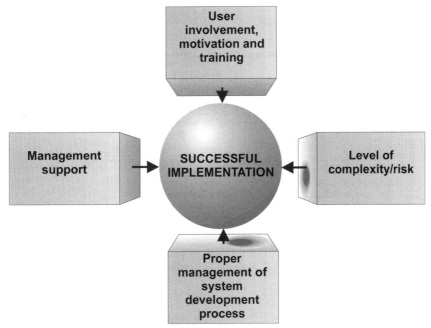

Figure 39.1: Factors in successful system implementation

These factors are considered in more detail below:

1. **User involvement, motivation and training.** If users are involved right from the start of a project, they have more opportunity to state their priorities and have some influence on the end result. Their expertise may lead to a better system being developed. Secondly, they are more likely to react positively to the finished system if they have had an active part in its development.

2. **Level of complexity and risk.** The larger the project, the greater the risk. Some projects are relatively straightforward and others are so highly complex that the requirements may change even before the project is completed. If the implementation team is inexperienced or lacks the required technical expertise, this adds to the likelihood of failure.

3. **Proper management of the system development process.** A project that is not properly managed is likely to suffer from:

   - Cost overruns;
   - Delays in completion;
   - Technical problems resulting in poor performance;
   - Failure to achieve expected benefits.

4. **Management support**. New systems that have the backing of management are more likely to succeed because they are more likely to be positively perceived by both users and technical staff. Also, sufficient funds are more likely to be made available. Changes in work habits and any organisational realignment associated with the new system are likely to be implemented more successfully with management backing.

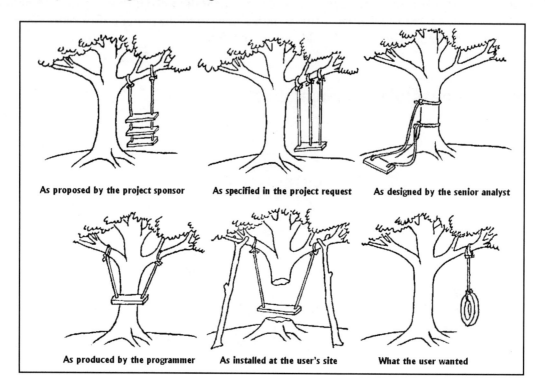

Figure 39.2: Problems of communication

Exercises

1. The management of a company wishes to introduce a computerised diary/scheduling package which is known to be compatible with the existing software base. With the aid of examples, give **three** factors which could influence the success or failure of this exercise. (6)

   NEAB IT04 Qu 2 1997

2. A theatre plans to introduce a computerised booking system. Apart from the ability to take bookings and print tickets, describe **two** other possible benefits to the theatre management. Describe briefly three ways in which the success of the new system can be measured. (5)

   New question

3. A company which distributes car parts has recently expanded and wants to commission a new corporate information system. It needs the system to be successful to ensure the future growth of the business.

   State **five** factors that could cause the failure of such an information system. (5)

   AQA ICT4 Qu 2 June 2002

4. Give **two** reasons why major information system projects which are scheduled to take several years to develop have a higher risk of failure than smaller ICT projects. (2)

   New question

Chapter 40 – Information Systems Strategy

Introduction

All businesses, from the smallest sole trader to the largest multi-national concern, need to have a long-term plan of where they are headed – a business strategy, in other words. Over the next few years, will the business expand or stay the same size? Will it develop new markets for existing products, or expand its product line? Should it aim to take over one or more of its supplier's or customer's businesses, or sell part of the business to a competitor?

Without a business strategy, a business may drift along for some time but it is unlikely to be successful in the long term. A strategy is needed for the following reasons:

- There needs to be an agreed set of objectives for the whole company so that the activities of individual departments are coordinated to serve these objectives.

- Resources have to be allocated to departments to buy new equipment, property and machinery, or to allow new products to be developed or advertised. Such expenditure can only be made effectively if there is an overall plan for the direction the business is moving in.

- Organisations have responsibilities to their 'stakeholders' – for example employees, owners, shareholders, banks and customers. The stakeholders will have a particular interest in seeing that the corporate strategy takes into account their interests.

A SWOT analysis (Strengths, Weaknesses, Opportunities, and Threats) may be used to identify internal and external factors that will have an impact on the business. (Figure 40.1)

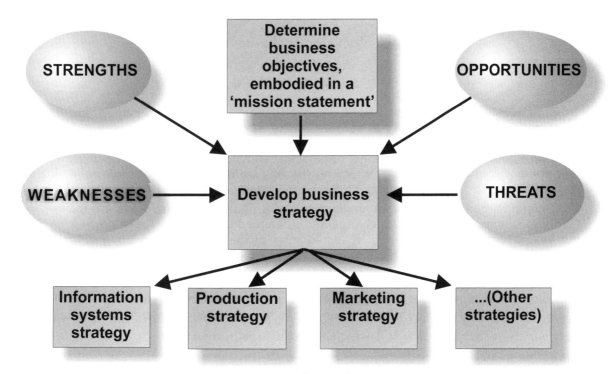

Figure 40.1: Formulating a business strategy

Formulating an information system strategy

An information systems strategy is just one part of the overall business strategy and must be developed within the context of the overall corporate objectives, which it will be designed to support. Expansion or development of an information system will inevitably involve:

- The allocation of significant resources;

- Changes in the way that certain parts of the business operate.

The emphasis in formulating the strategy is on determining the information needs of the business, rather than on how the information is to be provided. It must be led by the needs of the business and not by technology. However, an awareness of developments in technology will enable a business to find new ways of gaining competitive advantage.

The general organisational structure, the personalities of managers and other employees and the technology available will all play a part in determining the information system strategy.

Figure 40.2: Factors influencing an information systems strategy

The following is an extract from Ford's Graduate Recruitment brochure in 1998:

> **'Ford is looking for quantum improvements in cost, timing, productivity and customer satisfaction. The way to achieve this is through people, processes and technology. Most important are the people, because without a highly motivated workforce, willing to embrace change, none of this will happen. We need processes that are lean, robust and nimble, changing the way we do business, and we need leading edge technology to implement these processes.**
>
> **Our manufacturing and product engineering operations are two areas of the business undergoing significant change and Advanced Information Technology is the key to enabling that change. It is reducing cycle times, improving quality standards, and allowing us to respond more flexibly to changing customer needs.'**

➢ **Discussion: What impact does Ford's information systems strategy have on their recruitment strategy? What sort of people are they looking for in their Business Systems Department?**

➢ **What benefits do they hope that ICT will bring to the organisation?**

End-user computing

The 'end-user' is the person who uses the information produced by a management information system. Traditionally, the MIS professionals developed all the computer applications, and end-users were provided with the output in the form of reports. Today's computing environment is very different: end-users now typically develop systems themselves to satisfy a large proportion of their own informational requirements. For example, a manager may use a spreadsheet to work out the forecast for the next quarter. A marketing manager may develop a database application to help plan a marketing strategy for a new product. Teachers develop their own applications to track students' progress and print out results.

The management of end-user computing is one aspect of the overall MIS strategy of an organisation. The dividing line between what systems should be developed by the MIS professionals and what is more efficiently developed by the end-users themselves is not at all well-defined. Some managers think the best strategy is to exert strict control over end-user development (the 'monopolist' approach), while others see benefits in encouraging it to expand (the 'laissez-faire' approach). This allows the creativity and capabilities of end-users to be exploited to their full potential, and means that users' needs can be met without having to wait for funds or time to become available for a professional to develop or upgrade a system, or add a much-needed function to an existing system.

The policy also has major disadvantages:

- **Ineffective use of resources.** Many organisations spend more than half their total ICT budget on end-user computing, so cost-justification is essential.

- **Incompatible hardware and software between departments.** Hardware and software may be incompatible between departments. It is generally more economical to purchase a site licence for software than to have individual departments buying their own packages.

- **Poorly designed and documented systems.** Some systems may be developed by people who are less than expert in analysis, design and implementation, leading to systems which are difficult to use or allow invalid data to be input. Such systems may fall into disuse when the developer leaves.

- **Threats to data security and privacy.** Controls over what data is held, and who has access to it, may be missing.

ICT for competitive advantage

There are four major forces exerting pressure on a business:

- Bargaining power of customers;
- Bargaining power of suppliers;
- New and better products appearing which make the organisation's product obsolete;
- New competitors entering the market.

Figure 40.3: Pressures on an organisation

Strategies can be adopted to counteract these pressures, and maintain competitive advantage, for example by:

- Keeping costs lower than those of competitors;

- Producing better products than competitors;

- Creating new or different products that no one else produces;

- Locking suppliers or customers in to the organisation's products or services, for example by supplying excellent after-sales service.

➤ **Discussion: Information technology can help in all these aspects. Think of some examples of how technology can be used to keep costs down (see also case study below), or how it has been used in new products over the past ten years.**

Case study: Just-in-time at Wal-Mart's

Wal-Mart's is an American discount store that was among the first to use I.T. for competitive advantage in the 1980s. Many of Wal-Mart's strategies were born of necessity. 'Sometimes it was difficult getting the bigger companies – Proctor and Gamble, Kodak, whoever – to deliver to us, and when they did, they would dictate how much they would sell us and at what price', Walton said later. This forced him to set up his own distribution system. In 1969, with just 32 stores, he built his first warehouse so he could buy goods in volume.

In the past each store manager would order goods to replace those sold, relying on suppliers to deliver them direct to the shop – a hit-and-miss system that took up potential selling space for storage and often left shops out of stock. As Wal-Mart developed its distribution centres in the 1970s, it introduced two innovations. The first was 'cross-docking': goods were centrally ordered, delivered to one side of the distribution centre, and then transferred to the other side for delivery to an individual shop, along with the other goods the shop had ordered. This meant that one full lorry would make frequent trips to each store, instead of several half-empty ones visiting less often. To make this system work well, the firm had to keep track of thousands of cases and packages, making sure they were delivered to the right shop at the right time.

That was where computers came in. By the early 1980s Wal-Mart had not only set up computer links between each store and the distribution warehouse; through a system called EDI (electronic data interchange), it also hooked up with the computers of the firm's main suppliers. The distribution centres themselves were equipped with miles of laser-guided conveyor belts that could read the bar codes on incoming cases and direct them to the right truck for their onward journey. The final step was to buy a satellite to transmit the firm's enormous data load. The whole system covering all the firm's warehouses, cost at least $700m, but it quickly paid for itself.

The first benefit was just-in-time replenishment across hundreds of stores. This has since been refined further, using computer modelling programs to anticipate sales patterns. The second benefit was cost. According to Walton, Wal-Mart's distribution costs in 1992 were under 3% of sales, compared with 4.5 - 5% for the firm's competitors – a saving of close to $750m in that year alone.

Source: The Economist 4 March 1995

➤ **Discussion: Note how Wal-Mart's I.T. strategy was driven by its business strategies. What problems did Wal-Mart need to overcome to gain competitive advantage? In what ways does information technology help them?**

Exercises

1. Name **three** major resources of an organisation that will influence its business information strategy.
    (3)
    New question

2. An educational publishing company publishes about 100 different titles which are sold by direct mail and through bookshops. Describe briefly **three** alternative strategies which the company might adopt to increase its profit. For **each** of these strategies, show how information technology could help to carry them out.
    (6)
    New question

3. Describe briefly **three** factors within an organisation that can contribute to the successful implementation of an information system strategy.
    (3)
    New question

4. A national charity which provides housing for homeless people has a Head Office in London and 12 branch offices in other parts of the country. The management is currently developing an information systems strategy to help them achieve their objectives, which are to increase donations and ensure that the money raised is spent effectively. Describe briefly **four** ways in which information technology could be used to help them achieve their objectives.
    (8)
    New question

5. Name **four** external 'threats' to a commercial organisation, giving an example of each. Describe with the aid of an example in each case how information technology can be used to counteract these threats.
    (8)
    New question

6. The recruitment department of a large company has an MS Access database which was developed by an information systems professional, to help them keep track of students on sponsorship schemes.

    A student on the scheme is currently spending 3 months in the department and has found that there is a need for some extra reports, and that it would also be useful to keep details of sponsored students' 'mentors' on the database. As she recently gained a Grade A in Advanced Level ICT and acquired a good knowledge of Access in the process, she is able to add some extra options to the main menu, and also correct some minor bugs which have annoyed the recruitment personnel for some time.

    Describe, with reference to the above scenario, **two** advantages and **two** disadvantages of a management strategy that allows users a large degree of freedom to develop their own applications.
    (8)
    New question

Chapter 41 – Expert Systems

Definition

An expert system is a computer program that attempts to replicate the performance of a human expert at some specialised reasoning task. Also known as **knowledge-based systems**, expert systems are able to store and manipulate knowledge so that they can help a user to solve a problem or make a decision.

The main features of an expert system are:

- It is limited to a specific domain (area of expertise);
- It is typically rule-based;
- It can reason with uncertain data (the user can respond "don't know" to a question);
- It delivers advice;
- It explains its reasoning to the user.

An expert system has the following constituents:

- The 'knowledge base' that contains the facts and rules provided by a human expert;
- Some means of using the knowledge (the computer program, commonly known as the 'inference engine');
- A means of communicating with the user (the 'human-computer interface').

Uses of expert systems

Expert systems are used in a wide range of applications such as:

- **Medical diagnosis.**
- **Fault diagnosis** of all kinds – gas boilers, computers, power stations, railway locomotives. If your gas boiler breaks down, the service engineer may well arrive with a laptop computer and type in all the symptoms to arrive at a diagnosis, and then use the system to find out the exact part numbers of any replacement parts required for your particular model of boiler.
- **Geological surveys** to find oil and mineral deposits.
- **Financial services** to predict stock market movement or to recommend an investment strategy.
- **Social services** to calculate the benefits due to claimants.
- **Industrial uses** such as the expert system ELSIE described above.

Benefits of expert systems in organisations

Expert systems can be used to assist decision-makers in much the same way as an experienced colleague. They cannot entirely replace the decision-maker but they can dramatically reduce the amount of work that a person has to do to solve a problem.

Some of the *organisational* benefits of expert systems are:

- An expert system can complete some tasks much faster than a human – for example performing all the calculations required to estimate the costs of a construction project – which will enable an immediate response to be made to a client.
- A reduction in the downtime of an expensive piece of equipment when an expert system is able to quickly diagnose the fault.

- The error rate in successful systems is often very low and may be lower than that of a human being.

- Recommendations will be consistent: given the same facts, the recommendation will always be the same and completely impartial.

- An expert system can capture the scarce expertise of a well-qualified professional who may leave or retire, and can be used at locations where the human expert is not available – say, for geological surveys or medical expertise in remote areas.

- An expert system can be used as a repository for organisational knowledge – the combined knowledge of all the qualified experts in an organisation – which makes the organisation less dependent on an individual's knowledge, which may be lost when they leave.

- Expert systems can be useful for training employees.

Limitations of expert systems

- Expert systems can make mistakes, just as humans do, but even a low error rate in the diagnosis of a disease, for example, may cause people to mistrust a computer system.

- Expert systems do not 'learn from their mistakes' – new knowledge has to be entered into the knowledge base as it becomes available.

- It can be difficult to acquire all the required knowledge from the human experts in order to build the expert system. Expert systems work best when the problem is very well defined and the facts and rules associated with the problem can be clearly stated.

- The use of expert systems within an organisation can result in a decline in the skill level of some of the people using the systems. If a large part of the task is handled by an expert system, employees may not acquire the experience or knowledge that gives them a 'feel' for the task.

- Over-reliance on an expert system may stifle creative thinking and lead to the advice delivered being slavishly followed. For example an expert system which delivers advice on whether a client should be given a loan may come to a different conclusion from a human adviser who can spot exceptional circumstances that the expert system does not take into account.

➤ **Discussion: Southampton Football Club is experimenting with an expert system to decide on the monetary value of each player in the Club, based on number of goals, assists, contacts with the ball, age etc. It has been found to give a largely accurate estimate of the value of players who have been transferred in the past.**

➤ **What are the benefits to the management of using such a system? What factors are not likely to be taken into account by this system in assessing the desirability of selling or buying a player?**

Chapter 42 – Information

Introduction

The theme running through this entire course is information: ways of acquiring it, distributing it and using it at the various different levels of an organisation. In this chapter we'll take a closer look at the characteristics of information.

Sources of information

Information can be gathered from a number of different sources. It may be:

- Internal information produced by processing transactions within the organisation;
- External information collected by buying it from agencies or other organisations, reading trade magazines and newspapers, visiting trade shows, Internet databases, government and other statistics.

Levels of information

In the 1960s and 70s, computers were largely used for applications such as payroll, or for scientific and engineering applications where their ability to perform rapid and accurate calculations was an obvious benefit. But today, computers are invaluable because of the information that they can provide to assist and improve decision-making. There are three main reasons why information is needed in organisations:

1. A record of daily events and transactions must be kept so that the company can operate. For example, employees must be paid and records kept of gross pay, tax paid, pension payments and so on; customer orders must be recorded, invoices must be sent out and payments recorded, stock levels must be adjusted. This type of information is called **operational information**.

2. Middle managers in an organisation need information to help them manage effectively. For example, a supermarket manager needs to know how fast particular items move, how quickly stock can be replenished, how well a particular new product is selling, at what times of day or week the store is most crowded. This type of information is referred to as **tactical information**.

3. Historical information, environmental information and information about new businesses moving into the area may be used to build computer 'models' which help to forecast future changes or needs. For example, if a new car manufacturing plant is to open in a particular area, this may have an impact on local supermarkets because more workers and their families may move into that area. This type of information is referred to as **strategic information**.

Quality of information

Useful information should have certain attributes. It should be:

- **Brief.** The information needs to be as concise as possible: too much detail can result in overlooking vital facts. A stock report giving the amount sold and quantity in stock of every one of a hundred thousand items is not useful to a manager who needs to know which are the top selling items or the items which are not selling enough; a summary or aggregate of data is needed. Reports which only list items on which some action may be required are known as **exception reports**.

- **Accurate.** Information which is inaccurate is likely to lead to poor decisions being made and a loss of confidence in the source of the information. Sometimes information can only be given with a certain probability that it will be correct: for example, a farmer may rely on the weather forecast to plan when to harvest a field of wheat, but the forecast is unlikely to be 100% accurate.

- **Up-to-date.** Sometimes information needs to be up to the minute, for example in a booking system or ordering system where a customer needs to know whether a certain item is available. In other cases, it may not matter if the information is not up to the minute; a theatre manager reviewing the season's ticket sales does not necessarily need the figures for last night's performance.

- **Timely.** Reports must reach the right person at the right time.

- **Right level of detail.** Information is sometimes too detailed for a manager to be able to make sense of it. The principle of reporting by exception is very important in management information – in other words, only items that need some action on them are reported.

  Conversely, if not enough information is given it can be misleading. One of the criticisms leveled at the school League tables which are regularly published in newspapers is that they do not show how well a school performs in areas other than exam results – for example in creating a happy environment where each child fulfils his or her potential.

- **In an appropriate format.** Information can be useless if presented in a format which managers cannot understand. Sometimes a graph or chart may be a better way of presenting information than giving a list of figures.

> **Discussion: A manager in a fast food store wants to know how many days of sickness employees have had over the past 3 months. The data is available in the following form:**

REPORT FOR WEEK ENDING 13/12/97

Employee Name	Date	Hrs Scheduled	Hrs Worked	Reason for Absence
Andrews, M	10/12/97	7	7	
Andrews, M	11/12/97	5	4.5	
...				
...				
Goode, L	12/12/97	7	7.5	
Goode, L	13/12/97	8	0	Sick
...				

(rest of records for Goode, L followed by other employee records in alphabetical order)

> **Would this be a suitable report to present to the manager? What are its faults? Check the list given above for 'characteristics of good information' and suggest improvements.**

Case study: Clearing off to College

Every year thousands of students who fail to get the required grades for their chosen University place have to go through 'Clearing' to find a suitable place. This process is made infinitely easier by being able to look up information on the web site www.ucas.ac.uk . In 1999 between August 19 and September 8th the site received a mammoth 1.97 million hits, with over 20,000 students using the course search function to find places.

The key advantage online clearing has to offer is that information is constantly updated as course vacancies fill up and admissions grades alter.

Channels of communication

Formal information systems at an operational level are categorised by having well-defined procedures for the flow of data and information between the people who need it, often in the form of reports or other documents produced by the system. Sales orders in a manufacturing company, for example, may come in to the Sales Department, copies are passed to the Production Department, who will order parts from the Stock Department, who may need to order parts from a supplier, and so on.

How well data and information flows through an organisation will depend on several factors, including:

- The nature of the information – whether it is routine operational information or 'ad hoc' information requested intermittently by managers;

- The organisational structure – for example, the size of the organisation and the number of management 'layers';

- The amount of processing that has to be carried out on the data, and the frequency of processing;

- The geographical distance between the different parts of an organisation.

Case study: Guides need information

The Guide Association is a voluntary organisation with 700,000 members, one tenth of whom are adult leaders. Leaders are registered as members at one of nine regional offices in the UK Each region is responsible for the registration process, and each has a different PC custom-built member registration database system. There is a head office for the UK where programmes of activities and international events are developed for guides throughout the UK, and from which training for leaders is co-ordinated. This central office has no information on the membership because they are registered regionally.

The central office wants to provide more exciting opportunities to more members, and to be able to consult more widely with the membership at large. In order to achieve this and to plan for the future, there is a need to be able to access the regions' information.

Currently the central office has a Novell network, and is currently installing e-mail links to the regional offices. The regional offices have historically paid for their own ICT equipment, and therefore having taken advice locally, have all installed different hardware and software.

An ICT strategy is being developed which aims to improve communication and data sharing within the Association, and to enhance the management information available.

➤ **Discussion: What are the problems in getting the information to the Head Office of the Guide organisation? How can these problems be solved?**

➤ **Think of some ways in which the Head Office will be able to make use of the information it can access once the new system is in place.**

Presenting management information

The way that information is presented can be almost as important as the information itself. Information can be presented in numerous different ways:

- On computer printouts, using the principle of exception reporting for brevity and clarity;

- On a VDU. It could take the form of a report or a 'slide show' produced using a presentation graphics package, for example;

- Desktop published, incorporating company logo, graphs, diagrams, photographs etc;

- Orally – 'over the grapevine', by telephone or in formal presentations;

- Using videoconferencing to enable several people at separate locations to participate in meetings and information exchange;

- Over a company-wide intranet – an internal network which all employees have access to and on which important information can be posted.

> ➤ **Discussion: Think of other ways in which information can be disseminated to employees in an organisation.**

The intended audience

The way that information is presented will depend to a large extent on who it is intended to reach. Information on products and sales intended for customers will be presented in a different way from information intended for wholesalers or the company accountant.

Graphs and charts

Graphs and charts are an effective way of presenting information and highlighting problems or trends. A **bar chart**, for example, shows a trend at a glance. (Figure 42.1.)

Figure 42.1: Bar charts are often used in newspapers

A **line graph** may be a good way to highlight seasonal sales figures.

A **pie chart** can be a good way of showing how a total is made up, but is not effective if there are too many segments. The one shown in Figure 42.2 could be used to emphasise the amount of money spent on domestic services at Oxford Colleges.

Oxford Colleges		
Expenditure 1995/96		
	£m	%
Academic	33	29
Catering	10	8
Domestic services	30	27
Administration	13	12
Buildings	22	19
Other	6	5

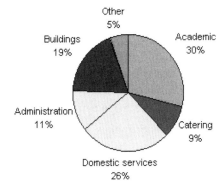

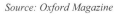
Source: Oxford Magazine

Figure 42.2: A pie chart illustrating a table of figures

Guidelines for presentations

A presentation could for example take the form of a talk accompanied by overhead projector transparencies or slides, or a slide show prepared in PowerPoint or a similar graphics package. Either way, the information on each screen or slide should be:

- Simple – no more than 5 or 6 clearly legible lines, in clear English;

- Brief – bullet points are a good communication tool;

- Visually appealing – don't use too many different fonts, or all uppercase letters. Graphs and charts are useful where numeric information has to be imparted.

Keeping everyone informed

The Department of Trade and Industry (DTI) commissioned a survey in 1997 of 'best practices' in over 100 different 'winning UK companies'. They note that in these organisations:

> 'Communication takes place in many directions throughout an organisation, and is always a two-way process. Just as the leaders of a company communicate their vision of where the company is going, they welcome and encourage feedback and ideas from all their employees, for they recognise that all have something to offer: "one proposal from each of our 100 employees is better than 100 proposals from one super boss". Communication takes the form of regular team briefings, frequent internal newsletters and regular contact with customers. In addition, senior management frequently gets out to meet employees by walking around the organisation and talking with individuals, encouraging the team concept of "us" rather than the divisive "them" and "us".'

Source: 'Winning' (A DTI report 1997)

The bar chart below summarises the different ways that information is disseminated around the organisations surveyed.

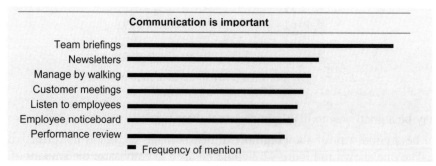

Figure 42.3: Methods of communication

Marketing information

One of the most valuable assets that many companies hold is the information they have collected about their customers. As well as names and addresses, they may collect information about their incomes, their professions, how much they spend, what products they are most likely to be interested in and so on. There are several ways this information can be collected:

- Every time a customer makes a purchase or orders a catalogue, their name and details are added to a customer database.

- When customers make a purchase and fill in a guarantee card, they are frequently asked to provide a lot of information about products they own, their income group, number of children and so on.

- People visiting a company's Web site can be asked to 'register' by providing a lot of personal information before gaining access to the site.
- Companies may buy mailing lists from other companies selling related products. For example, a company selling seeds, bulbs and shrubs may buy a list from a manufacturer of garden furniture.

Keeping a mailing list up-to-date is a major task – it is estimated that companies in the UK waste over £37m a year on 'gone-aways' – people who have died or moved with no forwarding address, and whose letters are returned. Companies do not usually remove 'gone-aways' from their lists: they mark them as such, and leave them on the database. If they subsequently buy a list from another organisation, they can run a program to identify names which appear on both lists, and thus avoid the problem of reinserting names they had previously deleted.

Some people object to their names being passed on, and questionnaires usually include a box to tick if the customer does not want this to happen. However, the data is often collected without the customer's knowledge, simply by making a purchase in a shop, so there is no guarantee that your name, address and purchasing habits are not on databases all over the world.

Exercises

1. The management of a company complains that the Management Information System (M.I.S.) continually fails to produce the appropriate information at the right time. The person responsible for the M.I.S. responds by blaming the 'inadequate data and information flow' within the company and requests a review of 'data and information flows'.

    (a) State **six** factors which influence the flow of information and data within an organisation.   (6)

    (b) With the aid of examples, describe **three** techniques which could be used to review the current information flows.   (6)

    NEAB IT04 Qu 8 1997

2. "The quality of management information is directly related to its timing."

    (a) Discuss this statement paying particular reference to:

    - The different purposes for which the information may be required;
    - The relative merits of speed versus accuracy.   (6)

    (b) In planning the information flow within a system, where are the delays likely to occur and why?   (6)

    NEAB IT04 Qu 9 Sample Paper

3. Many retail organisations have developed large databases of customer information by buying data from each other.

    (a) Describe **two** possible uses these organisations could make of the data they purchase.   (4)

    (b) Some customers may object to data held on them by one organisation being sold to another organisation. Describe some of the arguments which either of these retail organisations may use to justify this practice.   (4)

    NEAB IT04 Qu 2 Sample Paper

4. A manufacturing company intends to use an information system to store details of its products and sales. The information system must be capable of presenting the stored information in a variety of ways. Explain, using **three** distinct examples, why this capability is needed.   (6)

    NEAB IT02 Qu 4 1996

Chapter 43 – Data

Data capture

Data may be entered into a computer system by a variety of different methods depending on the quantity of data and the circumstances in which it is captured. Wherever practical, methods of direct data entry (without having to key data in) will be used to avoid the possibility of entering the data wrongly. Common methods of data include:

- bar code readers;
- magnetic stripe cards;
- smart cards;
- magnetic ink character recognition (for reading information from cheques – the amount still has to be keyed in);
- keyboard.

It is in some cases possible to avoid having to re-enter data that has already been captured by sending it from one organisation to another via Electronic Data Interchange.

Using bar codes

Bar coding is one of the most popular ways of capturing data, with the most common application being in shops and supermarkets where all items are bar coded. In spite of the high initial investment, it is estimated that a 2% investment of costs in information technology leads to a 6% saving in costs.

The major benefit of using bar codes at point of sale is that management is provided with very detailed up-to-date information on key aspects of the business, enabling decisions to be made quicker and with more confidence. For example:

- Fast-selling items can be identified quickly and automatically reordered to meet demand;
- Slow-selling items can be identified, preventing a build-up of unwanted stock;
- The effects of repositioning a given product within a store can be monitored, allowing fast-moving more profitable items to occupy the best space;
- Historical data can be used to predict seasonal fluctuations very accurately.

Bar code scanners are relatively low cost and extremely accurate: only about one in 100,000 entries will be wrong.

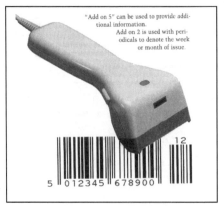

Photograph courtesy of Scanner Technologies

Figure 43.1: A bar code scanner

Other uses of bar codes

Bar codes can be used in a wide range of applications that require fast and accurate data entry. These include:

- **Warehousing**. Bar-coded containers of raw materials are stored in racks of bins which are also bar coded. When goods are put into the warehouse, the computer system instructs an automatic crane to retrieve the nearest available empty bin. The filled bin is then returned to an empty location. The crane relies entirely on bar codes to move goods in and out.

- **Transport and distribution**. All major road freight carriers now use bar codes. Individual packages are bar coded as are depot consignments. The exact location of any package is known at any one time together with details of the type of service used. Individual customers can be billed quickly and missing parcels traced more easily.

- **Manufacturing**. Very accurate data relating to work in progress can be obtained using bar codes as the data entry method. Management can obtain up to date data on the progress of unfinished goods, enabling bottlenecks and over-production to be reduced and production efficiency to improve.

- **Marketing**. Many polling companies now use bar-coded multiple-choice questionnaires to enter data quickly and accurately. Survey times can be dramatically reduced.

- **Medical**. Bar codes are commonly used to identify blood and other samples. Hospital patients' and outpatients' records are increasingly bar coded for fast retrieval and better accuracy.

- **Libraries**. Bar codes are used to record loans and provide more information on stock.

- **Banking, insurance and local government**. Bar codes are used extensively for accurate document control and retrieval. Many cheque book covers, insurance claim files and council tax forms are bar coded.

Magnetic stripe cards

Cards with a magnetic stripe are widely used for applications ranging from railway cards to customer loyalty cards. The information provided when someone signs up for a loyalty card with Sainsbury's, Tesco, Boots or W.H.Smith, for example, plus a few months of shopping records, can provide a detailed portrait of customers' habits.

The day is not far off when you will be able to wake up on Saturday morning (or whichever is your regular shopping day) to an e-mail from Sainsbury's suggesting what you need to buy this week.

Linking customers and suppliers through EDI

Electronic data interchange (EDI) is the electronic transmission of business data, such as purchase orders and invoices, from one firm's computerised information to that of another firm. Since EDI transmission is virtually instantaneous, the supplier's computer system can check for availability and respond quickly with a confirmation.

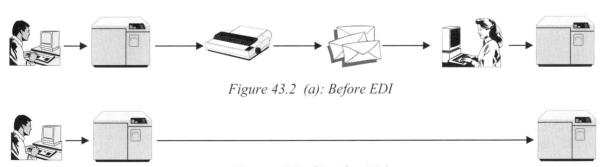

Figure 43.2 (a): Before EDI

Figure 43.2 (b): After EDI

Speed and reliability are major advantages of EDI. It does away with re-keying data, increases accuracy and eliminates delays. Data such as 'A' Level results are now commonly transmitted direct to schools and colleges rather than being sent by mail. Using a service such as BT's CampusConnect, schools and colleges are able to download the results in encrypted form up to two days before their official release date; at one minute past midnight on results day, they are sent a password which allows them to decode the results. Having the results on computer also makes it far easier for the schools and colleges to collate exam results and produce the various statistics and performance indicators required by the DfEE for national league tables.

Smart cards

Smart cards containing a microchip are likely to replace cash over the next five years. Cash-loaded smart cards are already undergoing trials in several British cities and university campuses.

Case study: A smarter way to pay

Students at Aston University are all issued with a plastic smart card. That one card gets the students through security checks into any area they need to visit. It can also be used to buy lunch at any one of the campus refectories or bars and acts as a student ID and library card.

If a student's cash balance gets low, it can be replenished at a bank or through a hole-in-the-wall machine that acts like a cashless ATM. There is a £5 minimum and £100 maximum cash capacity on the card.

➢ **Discussion: As students move around the campus, data can be collected about where they have been, what they have bought, what books they have borrowed from the library and so on. This data could be processed in many different ways to provide all sorts of management information. Think of some useful reports that could be produced, and ways in which this information could be used.**

➢ **What would be the benefits and drawbacks of smart cards replacing cash in the UK? It would theoretically be possible to know exactly how much cash each individual spent – would this be desirable, or an invasion of privacy?**

Keying in data

The keyboard is still widely used for data input in spite of the drawbacks of inaccurate data transcription (copying from a paper form), comparatively slow data entry and the risk to the health of employees who spend all day at a keyboard.

Banks, for example, no longer process routine transactions (such as paying in cheques) in branches. Instead, the work is sent to giant processing centres where the staff do nothing but key in data.

"It's like a factory", said one Barclay's worker. "There's just crates and crates of work everywhere. They call them customer service centres, but you never see a customer".

The trend is raising health and safety concerns among the banking unions. Four employees at one Midland Bank processing centre are currently taking their employer to court claiming they developed repetitive strain injury (RSI) after being required to key in 2000 cheque details per hour.

In order to ensure the accuracy of the data entered, it is commonly **batched** and **verified** – that is, entered twice by different operators with the second version being automatically compared with the first version and any discrepancies brought to the operator's attention. (See **batch processing** in Chapter 24.)

Other high volume data entry applications include processing results of customer research questionnaires. (See case study below).

Case study: Bradford & Bingley

In January 1998 the Bradford and Bingley, Britain's second biggest Building Society, mailed a questionnaire to its two million members asking them for personal details about their employment status, financial position and so on. Customers were also asked whether they agreed or disagreed with the statement "I appreciate the value of the long-term benefits provided by a mutual building society as against a one-off windfall from a converting society."

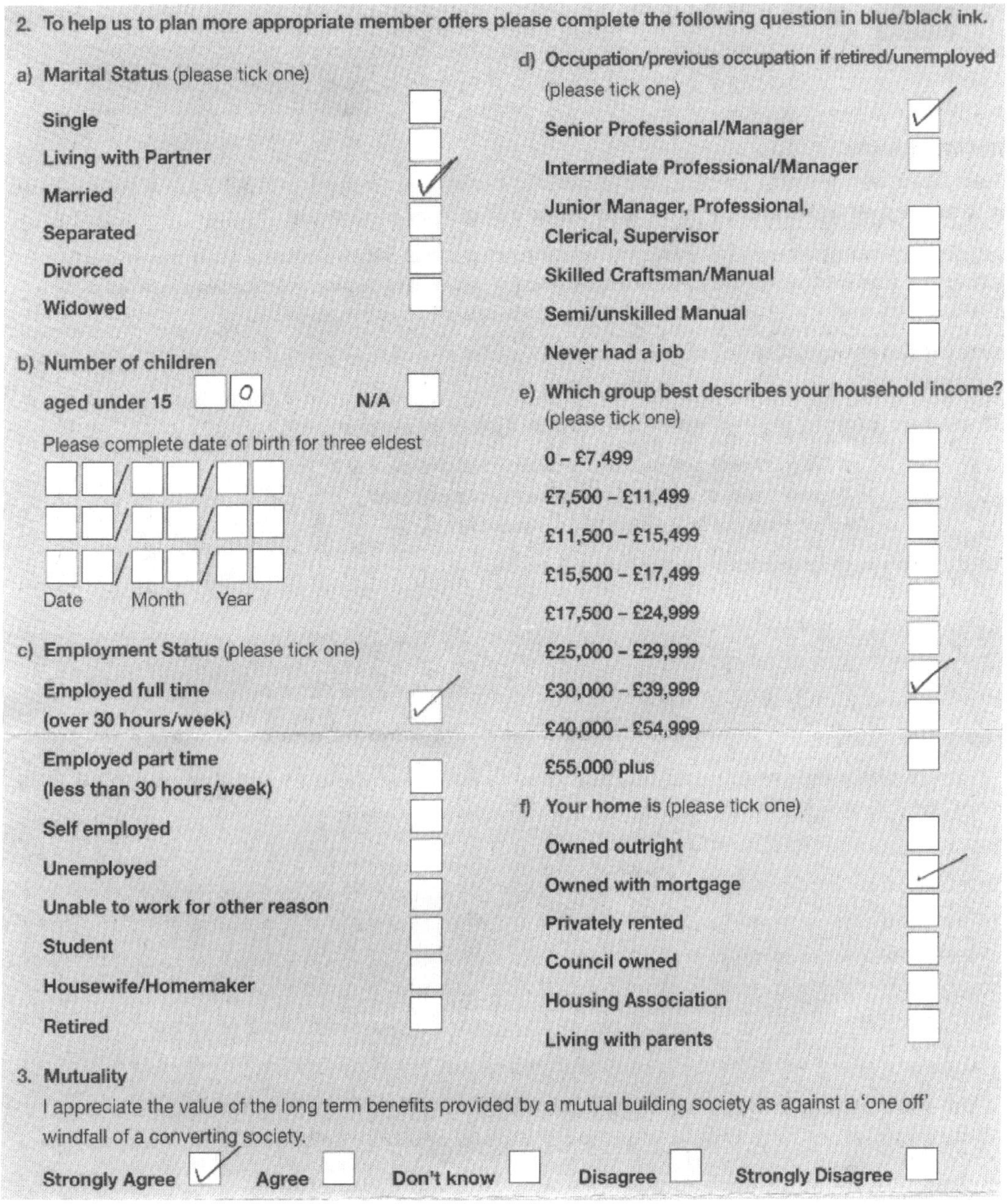

2. To help us to plan more appropriate member offers please complete the following question in blue/black ink.

a) Marital Status (please tick one)

Single
Living with Partner
Married
Separated
Divorced
Widowed

b) Number of children aged under 15 0 N/A

Please complete date of birth for three eldest

Date Month Year

c) Employment Status (please tick one)

Employed full time (over 30 hours/week)
Employed part time (less than 30 hours/week)
Self employed
Unemployed
Unable to work for other reason
Student
Housewife/Homemaker
Retired

d) Occupation/previous occupation if retired/unemployed (please tick one)

Senior Professional/Manager
Intermediate Professional/Manager
Junior Manager, Professional, Clerical, Supervisor
Skilled Craftsman/Manual
Semi/unskilled Manual
Never had a job

e) Which group best describes your household income? (please tick one)

0 – £7,499
£7,500 – £11,499
£11,500 – £15,499
£15,500 – £17,499
£17,500 – £24,999
£25,000 – £29,999
£30,000 – £39,999
£40,000 – £54,999
£55,000 plus

f) Your home is (please tick one)

Owned outright
Owned with mortgage
Privately rented
Council owned
Housing Association
Living with parents

3. Mutuality

I appreciate the value of the long term benefits provided by a mutual building society as against a 'one off' windfall of a converting society.

Strongly Agree Agree Don't know Disagree Strongly Disagree

Figure 43.3: A customer research questionnaire
(Reproduced with permission from Bradford & Bingley Building Society)

> ➤ **Discussion: What would be the best method of inputting data from the returned questionnaires?**
>
> ➤ **Studies have shown that on average one error occurs every 300 key presses. If the data is keyed in, approximately what percentage of forms will contain an error? Do these errors matter? How can they be spotted and corrected?**
>
> ➤ **What sort of analyses could be performed on the data to provide management with useful information about their customers? How could the management use this information?**

Exercises

1. A college collects data from incoming students which includes the students' subjects and grades at GCSE level. These grades are processed and used to predict an expected grade at A level. It is found that some of the grades given by students are less than accurate. Describe methods of data capture and entry which minimise this problem. (6)

    NEAB IT04 Qu 5 Sample Paper

2. A large supermarket has fifty checkout points. Each is equipped with a point of sale incorporating a bar code reading device and is linked to a computer in the stock room.

    The supermarket is one of a number of similar supermarkets, all supplied from a central warehouse.

    Each night the supermarket's computer is connected to the computer in the warehouse to pass on the requirements for the supply of stock.

    Fresh food is ordered direct from local suppliers each day according to demand.

    (a) (i)   Identify **three** points at which data is captured for this system.

    (ii) Describe **two** methods of capturing this data. (5)

    (b) Explain why the supermarket management might encounter difficulties if it relies only on sales data captured at the point of sale, as a basis for restocking the shelves. (2)

    (c) Occasional failures of equipment occur which might affect:

    • Point of sale terminals;

    • The supermarket computer;

    • The communication links;

    • The warehouse computer.

    Discuss how the system could be designed to cope with failures, without causing a serious loss of data, or making it impossible for the supermarkets to operate. (8)

    London Computing Paper 1 Qu 9 1997

3. Puregreens, a retailer of organic vegetables, have recently launched a marketing web site. The e-mail response from the "contact us" button has been overwhelming, so they are thinking of expanding into selling on-line.

    Discuss the implications of this, paying particular attention to the following:

    • Methods of data capture that will be available for on-line or off-line payment;

    • The control and audit issues associated with this method of selling;

    • The information needs of the management of this system;

    • The additional information that might be generated.

    The Quality of Written Communication will be assessed in your answer. (20)

    AQA ICT4 Qu 9 January 2003

Chapter 44 – The Management of Change

Outcomes from ICT investments

A study carried out in the UK in 1996 by OASIG, a special interest group concerned with the organisational aspects of ICT, came to the following alarming conclusions:

- 80-90% of systems do not meet their performance goals;
- About 80% of systems are delivered late and over budget;
- Around 40% of developments fail or are abandoned;
- Fewer than 40% fully address training and skills requirements;
- Fewer than 25% properly integrate business and technology objectives;
- Just 10-20% meet all their success criteria.

Source: OASIG Study 1996

This study drew on the expertise of leading management and organisational consultants and researchers, and covered approximately 14,000 organisations in all major sections of the economy, including a comprehensive range of ICT systems.

Valuing the workforce

The increasing complexity of interactions between business, work and technological changes is a source of an immensely difficult set of problems for everyone who manages, uses and develops ICT systems. These complexities are made even more difficult to resolve when organisations are faced with competitive and economic pressures. The emphasis on minimising costs and increasing efficiency sometimes means that not enough weight is given to other values and goals, and insufficient attention is given to human and organisational factors.

When cost savings are the dominant criteria on which ICT investments are judged, people become perceived as costs rather than as assets; as units of production rather than motivated beings who add value to products and services; as sources of error rather than assets whose experience and creativity differentiate one organisation from another.

Job cuts, described euphemistically as 'downsizing' or 'delayering' are often perceived as a major goal of a new ICT project. Naturally, employees are unlikely to participate enthusiastically in a new system that they perceive is a one-way ticket to unemployment.

Reasons why ICT systems fail

Common causes of the failure of new ICT systems are:

- There is too much emphasis on technological factors and the capabilities of the latest hardware. Trying to use the latest hardware, unproven by time and the experience of other organisations, is very risky.
- Senior managers are often vague about exactly what the objectives of a new system are. They may fail to understand fully the business opportunities and the difficulties arising from new ICT systems, justifying the investment on the grounds of cost reduction alone.

- This narrow viewpoint means human and organisational factors are often ignored. The way things are done and the jobs of individual users will be changed and this needs to be carefully explained and managed. Most senior managers do not have a good enough understanding of the links between technological and organisational change.

- Users are often not involved or invited to participate in the design or development of a new system and as a result are resentful and obstructive when they could make the difference between success and failure.

- Users may have been given unrealistic expectations of the new system so that even if it is a success judged by the performance criteria, they may be disappointed and feel that the effort was a waste of time. The benefits to the business may be overestimated by management, unintentionally or for political reasons.

- Costs are often underestimated.

- The time that the new system will take to develop is often underestimated.

- The new system may be over-ambitious. The more complex the system, the greater the risk of failure.

Case study: London Ambulance Service

It was never going to be easy computerising the largest ambulance service in the world, while at the same time profoundly changing an organisation that had existed since before the Second World War. Today, the service covers about 600 square miles with a population of 6.8 million residents, increasing steeply during the daytime. In January 1993 it employed 22,700 people including 200 managers and 326 paramedics. 300 emergency ambulances and over 400 patient transport vehicles struggled to cope with between 1,300 and 1,600 emergency calls a day.

In the early 1990s, the service was experiencing internal problems, with the staff resenting management's imperious attitude towards them, and management resenting the staff's resistance to change. In 1990 there was a major pay dispute and, in preparation for government health reforms, 53 senior and middle managers were made redundant. It was against this background of instability, organisational change and employee resentment that plans for a new computerised system were made. It was claimed that "it would be the first of its kind in the UK", and would involve "a quantum leap in the use of technology" – two phrases that should have caused a chill of foreboding in anyone remotely connected with ICT projects.

The objectives of the new system included the following:

1. Call-taking, accepting and verifying incident details, including location;
2. Determining which ambulance to send;
3. Communicating details of an incident to the chosen ambulance;
4. Positioning suitably equipped and staffed vehicles in places where they were most likely to be needed, so minimising response times to calls.

Under the manual process, when a 999 call was received the details were written down together with the location and a map reference. The form was put on a conveyor belt by one of the 200 people working in the department, and at the other end a resource allocator identified duplicate calls and, taking into account the location of ambulances from information radioed in, dispatched the nearest or most suitable one. The whole process took about 3 minutes.

Much of this process could be computerised, but part of the process depended on the judgement and experience of the dispatcher. But the end-users were not involved in the computerisation – there was little consultation of employees and many saw it as a way of downgrading their jobs and forcing them to accept unwelcome changes. They regarded it with distrust from the start. Training on the new system was given, but so far in advance of implementation (as the deadlines for implementation slipped) that many had forgotten how to use it by the time it was introduced.

In January 1992 a limited trial took place, which demonstrated a number of problems.

- Ambulance crews did not always report where they were and what call they were handling, and the computer required a perfect knowledge of where every vehicle was.

- Transmission blackspots and software error resulted in inaccurate location fixes of ambulances.

- The system could not cope with established working practices such as an operator allocating a different vehicle from the one allocated by the system.

- Problems with hardware, especially slow system response times during busy periods.

Despite recognition of all these problems, deployment of the full system went ahead on October 26 1992, with disastrous consequences. As the hours went by, the system knew the correct location of fewer and fewer ambulances. Neither did it know what equipment they carried or the particular skills of the crew on board. Several ambulances were dispatched to single minor incidents, and real emergencies were ignored. The staff had been told to minimise voice communications and lost complete control of the system. During the three-week period which followed, an eleven year-old girl died of renal failure after waiting 53 minutes for an ambulance. The irony was that she lived only two minutes from a hospital where she was a regular patient, and the only available ambulance was sent to a caller who turned out to have a headache.

The 80-page report which was produced after a three-month enquiry stressed that:

- such a system needs to be fully resilient and reliable, with fully tested levels of backup;

- the system must have total ownership by both management and staff, and staff must have confidence in its reliability;

- the system must be developed in a time scale and at a cost that allow for consultation, quality assurance and testing;

- the system should be introduced in a stepwise, modular approach;

- retraining of staff should be carried out thoroughly on the system, and the timing of the training should be such that 'skills decay' does not occur;

- a suitably qualified and experienced project manager should be appointed to ensure the close control and coordination of all parts of the system.

A full and fascinating account of this disaster is given in 'Crash' by Tony Collins.

➢ **Discussion: Change needs to be properly managed. What could the management have done differently to avoid this disastrous computerisation?**

Managing change successfully

Generally, the introduction of a major new ICT system needs to be preceded by a review of the organisational structure and current working practices. Trying to change too much at once is a sure step to disaster – and change cannot be successfully managed by imposing it on a reluctant organisation.

All the users of a proposed new system, from the shop-floor workers through to senior management, need to be involved and included in consultations. Ideas and misgivings should be listened to and proposed changes explained.

The benefits of a new system should be explained but not exaggerated – unrealistic expectations of what a new computerised system will do can lead to disappointment.

Training must be given to all those involved, not only in how to use the technology but also in the new organisational procedures and the consequences of not using the new system correctly.

Case study: Pindar

Andrew Pindar is the fourth-generation chairman of Pindar, a printing firm recently nominated as one of Britain's finest users of best-practice management. Pindar's main business is printing BT phone directories and industrial catalogues. Pindar described his early problems:

"Walking around Pindar, I encountered a feeling of frustration and dissatisfaction among the workforce. One could almost feel a certain hostility in the air, born no doubt out of a resentment and a feeling that management just did not understand the everyday issues and pressures heaped upon them by a hierarchy that never bothered to explain the logic behind directives. On the other hand, we had a management that could not understand why the workforce was not satisfied, in fact grateful, for being employed."

Andrew concluded that Pindar had to change, and he hired Time Manager International to put in place its Putting People First programme. Early enthusiasm soon dissipated, however. "I had a romantic notion that people would come along with me", he says, "and understand what we'd agreed at board and strategy meetings. I never appreciated that obstacles could be put in place, not by worker-bees, but by senior managers. They felt territory-threatened."

Pindar redoubled his efforts "My resolve was greater than their resistance." He staged the first of several all-worker conferences, and described how Pindar were putting in place foundations that would create maximum understanding, which would create commitment as their core philosophy.

The directories' workforce is a mixture of typesetters and graphic-arts graduates. Its database had a £1.5m upgrade a year ago, and now stores 300 billion bytes. "We are looking to replace it in October, with a £3m or £4m facility," says Rick Lumby, managing director of the Directories division. This will enable customers to dial into the Internet to amend ads.

Lumby says "When Pindar first got involved in technology in the early 50s, we had 20 employees. Now we have almost 1000. Has technology done us out of business? When we started doing telephone directories, we had 17 people working on them. We now have more than 200. Along the way, certain jobs have been automated out of existence. We've always changed for the sake of improving the job we do – because if we don't do it, somebody else will."

Source: John Lawless, Sunday Times 25 January 1998

➢ **Discussion: What factors contribute to the successful management of change at Pindar?**

Today's leaders, tomorrow's dinosaurs?

The coming of age of the Internet has posed enormous challenges to existing companies. At the same time it has given exciting opportunities to new companies which have been able to build up from scratch using the new technology. Thus it is not Waterstone's or WH Smith which is transforming the book business, but new companies such as Amazon and BOL. It is much harder for an established company to change because if they start to sell books over the Internet, this will adversely affect their High Street stores. Grabbing new opportunities threatens the value of their existing investments. On the other hand, if they do not change, they may be put out of business. So it was the newcomer, Direct Line, which transformed the insurance market rather than Guardian Royal or General Accident. These companies did not want to upset the insurance brokers who account for most of their business.

Many established companies are vulnerable: who needs banks, travel agents and shops like Marks and Spencer or Debenhams when you can get lower prices, better information and more choice from your armchair? In 1999, for example, 11% of all new cars in the US were bought on the Internet, and this is doubtless increasing every year. To many US car buyers, dealers are becoming simply pick-up points.

Managers have to adapt to this revolution or they will soon be logging on to www.unemployment.com.

Implications of change

The introduction of new technology or a change in the way an organisation does business will inevitably impact upon everyone in the organisation. Consideration will have to be given to:

- Possible redundancies and the effect of this on the rest of the workforce;
- Teaching and learning new skills;
- A change in organisational structure;
- Changes in employment patterns and conditions;
- Changes in internal procedures.

Exercises

1. An information system was introduced into an organisation and was considered a failure. The failure was due to the inability of the organisation to manage the change rather than for technical reasons.

   With the aid of examples describe **three** factors which influence the management of change within an organisation. (6)

   NEAB IT04 Qu 10 1997

2. It is not uncommon for designers involved in the introduction of information systems to encounter resentment and opposition from existing employees.

   Discuss the reasons for this response and describe steps that can be taken by the system designer to reduce this resistance. (10)

   NEAB IT04 Qu 10 Sample Paper

3. A small firm of solicitors is considering the introduction of an Information Technology system to improve the efficiency of its operations. One of the directors of the firm has expressed some concerns over the effects on the organisation of the introduction of the system.

   Describe **five** possible concerns the director may have, and the arguments that may be used to persuade her to accept the new system. (10)

   NEAB IT04 Qu 7 Sample Paper

4. New information and communication technologies are frequently introduced into companies as a result of outdated existing systems, market pressure, new legislation and other factors. Companies have to adapt quickly, or face going out of business.

   Discuss the factors that need to be considered to manage such changes successfully within an organisation. Particular attention should be given to:

   - Organisation structure and information needs;
   - Management and staffing issues;
   - Internal procedures, external procedures and the customer interface.

   Illustrate your answer with specific examples.

   The quality of written communication will be assessed in your answer. (20)

   AQA ICT4 Qu 9 June 2002

Chapter 45 – Security Policies

Threats to security and integrity

Today's organisations are dependent on their information systems, and most could not survive the devastating effects of their destruction. Threats to information systems include human error, computer crime, natural disasters, war or terrorist activities and hardware failure. (See Table 45.1)

Threat to security/integrity	*Example*
Human error	Mistakes in data entry Program errors Operator errors (e.g. loading wrong tape)
Computer crime	Hacking (unauthorised access) and stealing data Modifying data illegally Planting viruses or 'logic bombs' (code which remains inactive until triggered by an event such as a certain date becoming current, or an employee's record being marked 'Fired'.
Natural disasters	Fire, earthquake, hurricane, flood
War and terrorist activity	Bombs, fire, cyber-terrorist attack
Hardware failure	Power failure Disk head crash Network failure

Table 45.1: Threats to security of information systems

Risk analysis

"Those who think they have no time for bodily exercise will sooner or later have to find time for illness", said Edward Stanley, the 15th Earl of Derby. This quote could be paraphrased:

"Those who think they have no time or money to put in place a security policy will sooner or later have to find both the time and money for unplanned disaster recovery – and it will cost a lot more."

A corporate ICT security policy is a strategic issue, and as such is for company directors and senior managers to sort out, rather than something which can be left to technical staff. The first step in defining a security policy is to establish a clear picture of what the risks are and what the company stands to lose if disaster strikes. This **risk analysis** could include finding answers to questions such as:

- What is the nature of the data being stored in the system?
- How is the data used?
- Who has access to the system?
- How much money does the company stand to lose if the data is lost, corrupted or stolen?

Layers of control

Computer systems must be made secure to protect valuable data, and different 'layers' of security can be implemented, as shown in Figure 45.2.

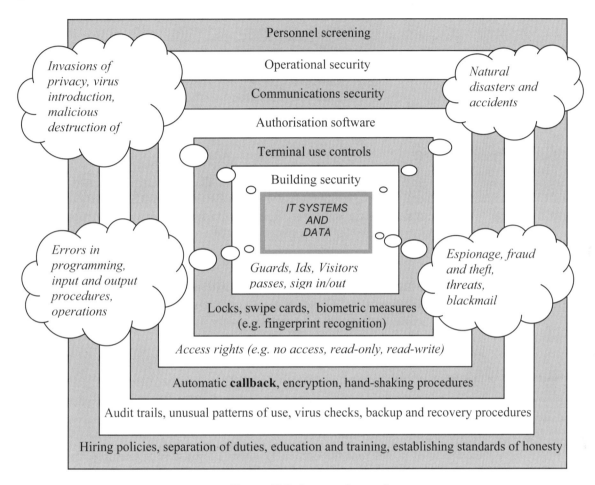

Figure 45.2: Layers of control

Building and equipment security

Building security can include measures to protect the premises from break-ins or unauthorised visitors, as well as from natural disasters such as fire and flood. Locks and window grilles, guards on the gate, rottweilers patrolling the fences, earthquake-proof construction, smoke alarms and automatic fire extinguishers are all possibilities.

Once in the building, even genuine employees and visitors may be restricted as to the areas they are permitted to visit. Employees may have ID cards with a bar code, magnetic strip or chip which allow access to particular areas. Visitors may be issued with passes. The visitor's pass shown in Figure 45.3 uses special ink which becomes visible 12 hours or so after being issued, and then displays 'EXPIRED' in red ink all over the card.

Biometric methods include fingerprint, handprint and iris recognition. These can be used to gain access either to a room or to a particular terminal. The Chancellor of the Exchequer, Gordon Brown, was presented in 1997 with a new dispatch box containing a laptop computer which required him to register a fingerprint before he could sign on. History does not relate whether he actually uses it.

Figure 45.3: A company visitor's pass

Authorisation software

Authorisation software includes the use of User Ids and passwords. The problem with passwords is that users tend to be careless with them – they use obvious words like FRED and PASSWORD, write down passwords, tell them to friends, and keep the same password for too long. A recent report on computer security revealed that for a number of years the chairman of a large company used CHAIRMAN as his password. Some companies insist that passwords are changed every month or so. Passwords are held on the computer system in encrypted form, with no way of decrypting them.

Access rights will be assigned to each user depending on their position in the organisation. A user may have different rights such as Read Only, Read-Write or No Access to different parts of a database. For example a worker in the Personnel Department may be able to change employee names and addresses but may not have access to salary details.

Communications security

Databases may be vulnerable to outside hackers. Methods of combatting such illegal access include **callback**, where the computer automatically calls back a predetermined telephone number when a user attempts to log in, **handshaking** and **encryption**.

A 'handshake' is a predetermined signal that the computer must recognise. For example, the computer may generate a random number and the user may then be required to multiply the first and last digits and add the product to the current month number. Of course this could pose a problem to people with shaky mathematical skills but it is generally more secure than a simple password, because it is never the same twice, and every user has their own algorithm.

Operational security

During daily operations, careful checks of logs showing terminal usage and any unusual behaviour should be regularly carried out. Many PC LAN security packages now include **audit controls**. Audit controls track what happens on a network, for example:

- which users have logged on, where from and for how long;
- how many times a server has been accessed;
- what software has been used;
- which files have been accessed by which users;
- how many unsuccessful attempts were made to log on from any terminal (to detect hackers trying to guess the password).

Anti-virus software can be installed on all PCs, and employees forbidden to bring in disks from outside the organisation. Viruses can also be introduced by downloading files from the Internet, so to guard against spreading a virus from one of these files, many firms run anti-virus software every night. This isolates all files containing a virus in a special directory and leaves a warning message on the screen.

Backup and recovery procedures form part of disaster planning which is discussed in the next chapter.

Audit trail

An **audit trail** is a record that allows a transaction to be traced through all the stages of processing, starting with its appearance as a source document and ending with its transformation into output.

Public companies have to have all financial records audited by external accountants every year, and the system must create an audit trail that makes it possible to see how each figure on a report is arrived at. No accounting system allows a financial record simply to be altered without a transaction being stored which can be checked. The auditor typically selects source documents, traces associated entries through intermediate computer printouts, and examines the resultant entries in summary accounts.

It is not only financial systems that have a use for audit trails, as the case study below illustrates.

Case study: Harold Shipman, GP and serial killer

Harold Shipman, a trusted family GP from Mottram, near Hyde, Greater Manchester was convicted in January 2000 of murdering 15 of his elderly female patients. This is a transcript of part of an interview between Dr Shipman and the detective at the police station after he was arrested.

"You attended that house at three o'clock and that's when you murdered this lady, and so much was your rush to get back that you went back to the surgery and immediately started altering this lady's medical records; we can prove that only minutes after three o'clock on that date you are fabricating that false medical history for this woman. You tell me why you needed to do that?"

"There's no answer."

"Well there is, there is a very clear answer because you've been up to her house, rolled her sleeve up, administered morphine, killed her and you were covering up what you were doing. That's what happened, isn't it, doctor?

"No."

"I am now showing you .. an exhibit .. from your computer which shows what's placed in, when and what's removed…"

The doctor examines the document. It shows that a patient record from August 1, 1997, a woman complaining of chest pains, accompanied by a doctor's note "?? angina", was actually typed into the computer three minutes and 39 seconds after the doctor had left the woman's house following her death on May 11, 1998.

"I'll ask you again, doctor, Where's that information come from?"

"I've no recollection of me putting that on the machine… I still have no recollection of entering that onto the computer… I'm well aware that that's how an audit trail works … there's no argument about that…"

Shipman has no answers now, except to say that the clock on his computer is not set for summer time and must be out by one hour.

The computer's audit trail helped to provide enough evidence to charge Shipman eventually with 15 murders – leaving another 131 other suspicious deaths to be investigated.

Source: David James Smith, The Sunday Times 6 February 2000

Personnel safeguards

Many studies show that users and computer personnel within an organisation are far more likely to breach security than outsiders. Security may potentially be breached by anyone from computer operators and programmers right up to company directors. Motivated by revenge, financial gain, fanaticism or irrational behaviour, employees are sometimes well-placed to plant a virus, steal or corrupt data, set up false accounts or attempt to extract money by extortion by threatening to destroy vital files.

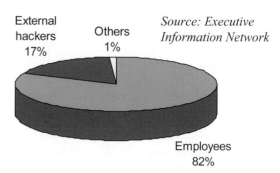

Figure 45.4: Who commits computer crime?

Motivating employees to be alert to security breaches and giving publicity to security measures may serve as a deterrent to computer crime.

Separation of duties is an important principle in maintaining security of data – no employee should perform all the steps in a single transaction. This makes it more difficult for a single individual to perpetrate fraud or theft.

Corporate ICT security policy

Once the risks to ICT systems and data have been established, policies can be determined which will be effective without costly overkill. There is often a conflict between wanting to make systems as secure as possible, but at the same time accessible to authorised users. For this reason university, college and school systems tend to be relatively insecure, because one of their most important requirements is to be easily accessible by students.

Once policies have been developed, they need to be implemented. The best security policy in the world is no use if people do not abide by it, and the key here is education – all employees should be made aware of the security policies and mechanisms put in place to ensure that they are adhered to. Instilling norms of ethical behaviour with respect to the use of information and information systems is an important management responsibility.

A typical security policy will cover the following aspects:

- **Awareness and education;**

    Training and education requirements

    Timetable for training/education

- **Administrative controls;**

    Formal procedures and standards are defined for all ICT systems

    Careful screening of personnel during the hiring process

    Separation of duties to ensure that it would take collusion between at least two employees to perpetrate fraud

    Disciplinary procedures in the event of security breaches

- **Operations controls;**

    Backup procedures

    Control of access to data centres by means of smart cards, ID badges, sign-in/sign-out registers

- **Physical protection of data;**

    Controlled access to sensitive areas

Protection against fire and flood

Uninterruptible power supplies

- **Access controls to the system and information;**

   Identification and authentication of users

   Password protection

   Different levels of access for different users according to their needs

   Different access rights, e.g. read only, read-write, read-write-update, etc.

   Encryption of sensitive data

   Detection of misuse using, for example, audit control software which detects multiple attempts to get a password correct.

- **Disaster recovery plan;**

   (See next chapter.)

Case study: War on the Web

Should we be more worried about terrorists using digital weapons rather than chemical and biological attacks? A cyber-terrorist attack on our 'critical information infrastructure' – the electronic systems vital for government, armed forces, business, finance, telecommunications, utilities, emergency services – could paralyse the country and bring all these systems to a grinding halt.

It is not hard to imagine that terrorist organisations are training and preparing hackers and virus writers around the world for a large-scale, coordinated assault that piles attack upon attack until systems fall over. It would be cheap and involve little risk of those involved ever being caught.

➤ **Discussion: Is there anything that organisations can do to protect themselves from cyber-terrorists?**

Exercises

1. A particular organisation uses a computerised stock control system. On performing the half-yearly stock check it is discovered that the actual stock levels of some of the items are below that shown on the system.

   (a) Describe the functionality which should have been built into the software to minimise the possibility of this happening. (2)

   (b) Explain why this functionality is required. (2)
   NEAB IT04 Qu 5 1997

2. Some software packages can be set up to monitor and record their use. This is often stored in an access log.

   Name **four** items you would expect to be stored in such a log. (4)
   NEAB IT04 Qu 1 Sample Paper

3. Many accounts packages have an audit trail facility. Explain why such a facility is necessary, what data is logged and how this information can be used. (6)
   NEAB IT04 Qu 6 Sample Paper

4. Describe briefly **four** areas you would expect to be covered in a company's security policy. (4)
   New question

Chapter 46 – Disaster Recovery

Effects of negligence

The risks to businesses from computer disaster range from spilling a cup of coffee into the computer file server or a workman drilling through a cable to a fire or bomb which completely destroys the building. The results of such an incidence may be catastrophic: a recent survey showed that about 90% of companies which suffered a significant loss of data went out of business within two years. Of these, 43% went out of business almost immediately.

After working for 1 day without essential business data, a company operates at about 96% of its capability. By the tenth day, it is operating at only about 10% of its capability (Figure 46.1).

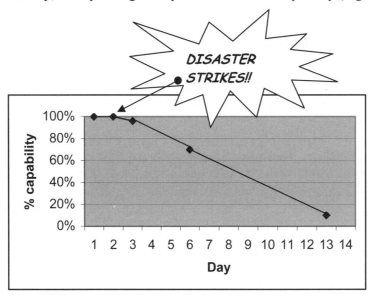

Figure 46.1: Effect of disaster

In the UK, the company and the directors may be prosecuted by the Health and Safety Executive if loss of essential business data or safety data adversely affects the health and safety of the public or the environment. In the case of banking, financial, insurance and related services, loss of essential business data which adversely affects the customer could bring about very costly litigation and fines.

> ➤ **Discussion: Suppose that a supermarket had all its data stored on disks and tapes in a computer room which was destroyed by a small localised fire one night. What sort of data would it have lost? Can you imagine the consequences? How long could it continue to operate?**

Stages in disaster planning

However many precautions are taken, no company can protect themselves completely against a disaster which will wipe out their computer system. What they must do is to ensure that if this happens, they can be up and running again in the shortest possible time. In disaster recovery planning, an essential task is to identify the most critical business functions to be supported by the plan, since covering less vital functions is, in general, too costly.

Contents of a security plan

The first step in solving any problem is understanding and defining it, and then assessing how it may affect the company. A security officer may be appointed who has both the technical and organisational skills to implement a security plan. The key elements of such a plan include:

- A list of the most critical business functions;

- A list of the facilities, hardware, software, data, personnel and other equipment that are necessary to support those functions;

- A method for securing access to all necessary resources;

- A method for getting in touch with all key personnel;

- A step-by-step course of action to follow to implement the plan;

- Education and training of personnel involved in implementing the plan;

- Regular drills to test the effectiveness of the plan.

Disaster recovery plan

Two 'controls of last resort' can be put in place to guard against the failure of a business after a catastrophe – adequate insurance and a disaster recovery plan.

Insurance is not a substitute for loss prevention, and it cannot lessen the likelihood of loss – it can only help to reduce the financial impact of such a loss when it does occur. Insurance premiums will be based in part on the precautions that the company has taken to protect itself against disaster.

A disaster recovery plan has to contain provision for backup facilities which can be used in the event of disaster. Three alternatives are:

- A company-owned backup facility, geographically distant from the main site, known as a 'cold-standby' site.

- A reciprocal agreement with another company that runs a compatible computer system.

- A subscription to a disaster recovery service, such as the one described in the case study below.

Case study: Trust in the Virtual World

Ron Hixon says of his workforce: "I trust them, that's the key." Yet none of those 70 employees has turned up at the office. They will not be in the office tomorrow, either. As he looks round his 6000sq ft of almost deserted premises in Woking, Surrey, he is untroubled.

His staff are computer technicians who work from home. With a modem and a laptop, they are connected to the rest of the company as surely as if they were in the room next door. Mr Hixon's company, Catalyst Technology Solutions, is a service provider to the service sector, providing disaster recovery services for businesses. If a client is hit by fire or flood, or a computer malfunction, they can reload their companies' data onto the Catalyst system and continue to operate as if the crisis had never happened.

The Woking office stands empty, so if a client's premises have been destroyed, they can move in their whole operation. The paradox of running a company with 30,000sq ft of empty office space on three separate sites, and 70-plus employees who work from home appeals to Mr Hixon, who has further plans for revolutionising Catalyst. A new telephone system will soon automatically route calls to workers' home numbers or another location, and divert them to a secretary if the call is unanswered.

"Customers will think they are talking to an office full of people, whereas in fact we could be anywhere."

Meanwhile the offices stay empty, waiting for disaster to strike, while the virtual workforce talk to each other through the ether.

Source: Charlotte Denny, The Guardian 25 August 1997

> ➤ **Discussion: Can you think of some local organisations which would need to make use of a disaster recovery service such as this if they experienced a catastrophe?**

Criteria used to select a contingency plan

The choice of contingency plan will be based upon the costs of the extra provision vs. the potential cost of disaster. Factors which will be taken into account include:

- The scale of the organisation and its ICT systems;

- The nature of the operation: an on-line system may need to be restored within hours, whereas a customer billing operation may not be unduly harmed by a few day's delay, so long as no data is lost;

- The relative costs of different options: a company with several sites linked by telecommunications may be able to formulate a disaster recovery plan which temporarily moves operations to an alternative site, but need not involve a special 'cold-standby' site, or a 'hot' site provided by a third party;

- The perceived likelihood of disaster occurring: companies in the earthquake zone around San Francisco, for example, are likely to invest more in a disaster recovery service than the average firm in Ipswich.

> ➤ **Discussion: What are the most critical ICT functions at your school or college? What would be the consequences of a disaster such as fire or theft of computer equipment? What sort of contingency plan would be appropriate?**

Exercises

1. A small company runs a network of 4 PCs on which it keeps records of stock, customer accounts, a mailing list and a multitude of word-processed documents. Draw up a security plan for this company to ensure that it will be able to continue operating normally within a day or so of a disaster such as a fire. (20)
   New question

1. A growing organisation has realised that so far they have been lucky in that their information systems have not failed. Before they expand their business operational reliance on ICT, they have been advised by their insurer to carry out a risk analysis and then plan what to do next.
   (a) Explain what is meant by risk analysis. (3)
   (b) State **three** different potential threats to an information system, and describe a counter measure for each one. (9)
   (c) Describe **three** of the criteria that could be used to select a disaster contingency plan. (6)
   AQA ICT4 Qu 8 January 2003

3. Briefly describe the safeguards a company could use against each of the following threats to its computer system.
   (i) Terrorist bomb;
   (ii) Accidental overwriting of a master file;
   (iii) Hackers outside the organisation;
   (iv) A corrupt employee perpetrating fraud; (8)
   New question

Chapter 47 – Implementation of Legislation

Laws relating to ICT

Legislation governs many aspects of the use of computers within organisations, and it is the responsibility of organisations to ensure that the legislation is implemented. The laws include:

- The Data Protection Acts of 1984 and 1998. (see Chapter 12);
- Copyright Designs and Patents Act of 1988 (see Chapter 10);
- The Health and Safety (Display Screen Equipment) Regulations of 1992 (see Chapter 13).

The Data Protection Act

The Data Protection Act exists to protect the privacy of individuals, its main areas of concern being that:

- Data and information should be *secure;*
- Private, personal or other data should be *accurate;*
- Data stored should not be *misused.*

Organisations should develop their own privacy policies to ensure that the law on Data Protection is upheld. A policy might typically contain two sections, one focussing on the customers and the other on the organisation itself.

A data protection policy

Section 1: Customer Service

1. The policy on data privacy should be publicized, and customers given a copy on request.
2. Customers should be told why their personal information is needed and what use it will be put to. No more data than is necessary should be collected.
3. Data should be obtained directly from the customer, to ensure as far as possible that it is accurate.
4. No data should be used for any purpose other than that which it was collected for, without the customer's consent. This includes selling the data to a third party.
5. Consent should be obtained by providing a clear opt-out check box on any form used to collect data.
6. Customers should be given easy access to files containing their own personal information.
7. Any errors in personal data should be corrected immediately.
8. Customers' concerns should be listened to and acted upon.

Section 2: Organisational culture

1. The company's policy should be clearly communicated to all staff. The policy may form part of a company handbook, form part of a training program, or be posted on notice boards or an Intranet.
2. An awareness of the issue of privacy should be fostered among all employees.
3. Staff should be held accountable for the company's privacy policy. It should be emphasised that if an individual acts contrary to a clause of the Data Protection Act, the individual is personally liable.
4. The effect on privacy of any new proposed system or service should be assessed before it is developed.

5. Reasonable steps should be taken to ensure that all data stored or used is accurate and up-to-date.

6. A schedule should be kept of how long data can be stored before it should be destroyed.

7. A security policy should be developed and enforced to ensure that all data is kept secure from accidental or malicious damage and from unauthorised people looking at it.

8. A senior manager should be designated to be responsible for seeing that the security policy is enforced.

9. All staff should be made aware of their responsibilities to keep data secure by keeping passwords secret, changing them regularly, maintaining physical security of disks, performing scheduled backups etc.

10. Periodic checks should be made to ensure that the policy is being adhered to.

Software copyright

Under the terms of the Copyright Designs and Patents Act of 1988, it is illegal to copy software or run pirated software. The Business Software Alliance (BSA) exists to make organisations and their employees aware of the Law and steps they should take to ensure that it is implemented.

Figure 47.1: The Business Software Alliance provides guidance to companies

The BSA has prepared a step-by-step guide to software management which includes the following advice:

- **Conduct an audit.** Prepare an inventory of your current software situation by conducting an audit using a commercially available audit tool or commissioning an audit service provider. Any illegal software discovered during the audits should be deleted immediately.

- **Purchasing.** Purchase licences for enough copies of each program to meet your current needs. Network operators should consider purchasing a network metering package to restrict the number of users according to the number of licences.

- **Procedures.** Demonstrate your organisation's commitment to using legal software by adopting the following procedures:

  - Appoint a Software Manager to ensure that all appropriate software analysis and management functions are conducted efficiently.

  - Arrange an audit of all machines on a regular basis.

  - Send a memo to all staff reiterating your organisation's concerns about software duplication and advising them of the forthcoming audit. (See Figure 47.2)

- Channel software requirements/purchases through a single point. One of the main entry points for unscrupulous resellers is through a fragmented purchasing system in which various personnel are ordering software.

- Make regular checks on software suppliers and software entering your company.

- Send a memo to staff, and add a note within your company policy and employee handbook, that illegal software copying is a disciplinary offence and that piracy should be reported.

- Request your staff to sign an employee agreement verifying their understanding of the organisation's policy regarding the use of illegal software.

SUGGESTED MEMORANDUM TO EMPLOYEES

To: (Specify distribution)

From: (Senior management official or CEO)

Subject: PC software and the law

Date: (insert)

The purpose of this memorandum is to remind you of (name of organisation)'s policy concerning copying and use of software.

Unlicensed duplication or use of any pirated software program is illegal and can expose you and the company to civil and criminal liability under copyright law.

In order to ensure that you do not intentionally or inadvertently violate copyright, you should not copy any program installed on your computer for any purpose without permission from (insert reference to responsible manager or department). Likewise, you should not install any program onto your computer without such permission, in order to verify that a licence is held to cover such installation.

- The company will not tolerate any employee making unauthorised copies of software.

- Any employee found copying software illegally is subject to termination from the company.

- Any employee copying software to give to any outside third party, including clients and customers, is also subject to termination.

- If you want to use software licensed by the company at home, you must consult with (insert name of manager) in order to make sure such use is permitted by the publisher's licence.

Figure 47.2: A sample memo to staff

Education of employees and a raising of awareness of the problems and consequences of software piracy is a major step in controlling software misuse.

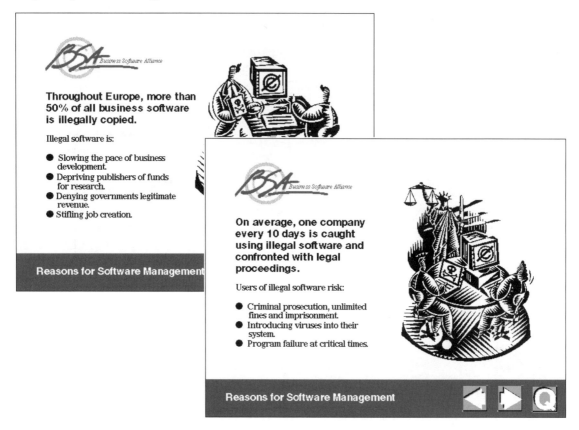

Figure 47.3: Part of a BSA presentation

Health and Safety

Where health is concerned, prevention is always better than cure and the first step is to understand why and how health complaints associated with computer use begin. Measures can then be taken to avoid the bad habits, unsuitable equipment and furniture and poor working environments that are frequently to blame.

Whether people are using computers at home or at the office, the way they interact with their computer affects their physical and mental health. Educating employees and instilling good working practices is one way of preventing problems such as backache, eyestrain and repetitive strain injury (RSI).

Employers should avoid incentive schemes designed to increase the rate of data entry, as applying pressure of this sort has been shown to contribute to the onset of RSI (see case study "Bank staff driven to injury" in Chapter 13).

Encouraging 'ownership' of workspace

Under the Health and Safety at Work Act, employees have a responsibility to use workstations and equipment correctly in accordance with training provided. They are also required to bring any problems to the attention of their employers and cooperate in their correction. One way that employers can help to ensure that employees heed this directive is to involve them in the choice of furniture, hardware and software, as well as in the arrangement of the office space. People generally are better motivated and take a more responsible attitude if they are consulted and allowed to define their own workspace.

Taking regular breaks

Specialists recommend thirty-second 'micropauses' every five to ten minutes, with longer pauses of ten to fifteen minutes every hour or so. Providing regular breaks and coffee-making facilities, as well as varying tasks, can help prevent health problems. Employers who provide this kind of environment are also likely to end up with happier and more productive employees.

Providing the right equipment

There are regulations concerning the type of computer equipment and furniture that must be provided for people who spend a lot of time in front of a VDU. Refer back to Chapter 13 for guidelines on the ergonomic environment.

The employer's responsibility

Employers are responsible for the health and safety of their employees, and they are obliged to demonstrate this responsibility by carrying out a formal evaluation of the working environment and acting on any feedback from the evaluation. This evaluation should either be carried out by an employee whom the Health and Safety Executive recognises as competent, or by an independent professional ergonomist, and it will cover workplace design, including computer hardware, lighting, cooling, humidity and software.

The bottom line is that ignorance of the law is no defence, and sooner or later all organisations will have to invest some money in ergonomics. Companies who disregard their obligations may be successfully sued by injured employees.

> ➤ **Discussion: Does your computer classroom satisfy the ergonomic requirements of the Health and Safety legislation? Does the school or College have an obligation to comply with the terms of the Directive?**

Exercises

1. A Company uses a computer network for storing details of its staff and for managing its finances. The network manager is concerned that some members of staff may install unauthorised software onto the network.

   (a) Give reasons why it is necessary for some software to be designated as unauthorised. (2)

   (b) What guidelines should the network manager issue to prevent the installation of unauthorised software onto the network? (2)

   (c) What procedures might be available to the company to enforce the guidelines? (2)

   NEAB IT04 Qu 6 1997

2. A particular college uses a computer network for storing details of its staff and students and for managing its finances. Network stations are provided for the Principal, Vice-Principal, Finance Officer, clerical staff and teaching staff. Only certain designated staff have authority to change data or to authorise payments.

   (a) What are the legal implications of storing personal data on the computer system? (4)

   (b) What measures should be taken to ensure that the staff understand the legal implications? (3)

   NEAB IT03 Qu 3 Sample paper

Chapter 48 – User Support

The need for support

As computers become more and more powerful, the software that runs on them becomes more and more sophisticated. The 'ease of use' promised by graphical user interfaces like Microsoft Windows has made PCs accessible to more and more non-technical users, so that paradoxically the need for user support is set to continue growing, rather than the reverse. The nature of the support services required by users has also changed since the days of terminals running a single, character-based application: the more features and complexities there are built into the software, the more expertise is required to solve users' problems.

Software companies which create tailor-made ICT solutions for companies, as well as manufacturers of software packages, all provide user support, though users are normally expected to pay an annual fee for this service, whether or not they use it.

The help desk

User support may be provided in a number of ways, from a simple help desk to a user support centre. The person sitting at the help desk answers telephone queries during office hours and depending on their skill level, attempts to solve the problem or passes it over to an expert. There may be other ways of contacting the help desk such as fax or e-mail, but essentially this is a receive-only service, existing to take queries and resolve them.

The help desk offers a single point of contact for customers, and a good rapport can be built up between the person on the help desk and the customers. All the questions asked by different customers can be stored on a database and this can provide useful information about the usability of the software. The information can then be used to improve future versions of the software or plan training courses.

On the other hand, the work can be demoralising for the person at the help desk, especially if they generally have to pass the problem on to someone else to solve. People typically only call a help desk as a last resort, by which time they are probably quite frustrated and angry and ready to take it out on whoever picks up the phone. Communication can be a problem when the help desk tries to explain the problem to a third party, and quite probably the problem solver will not see the problem as a top priority so that the service may not be very fast or efficient.

The help desk will typically log:

- The user's name and telephone number or postcode;
- Version number of the software;
- Serial number of the software (to ensure that the user has a legitimate copy);
- The nature of the enquiry;
- The time and date of the call.

Using e-mail rather than the telephone is sometimes cheaper and avoids the problem of a telephone line that is constantly busy. Being held in a queue of callers for half an hour or more is not uncommon on the average help line, and it's bad luck if you don't like the music they've chosen to play you while you wait.

Technical support

Technical support exists to solve technical problems and tends to be staffed by specialists who perhaps had some hand in writing the software, but have very little idea of how the software is used in a business context. There may be problems of communication between the expert spouting technical jargon and the business user who wants to know how to get the package to allocate, say, a different level of discount to a particular customer.

Help desk software

Special help desk software such as McAfee's HelpDesk Suite is available for large and small organisations running a help desk.

This software comes with an Expert System database of answers to over 25,000 different hardware and software problems, which enables the staff at the help desk to ask the right questions and let the software diagnose the problem. It also allows the helper to take over the user's computer and screen, calling it up on his own screen and typing in the necessary fix. A 'whiteboard' facility allows all users within an organisation to be notified of a particular problem – say, the printer in a particular area is not functioning, or the network will go down between 5pm and 7pm on Tuesday. Numerous reports are available, for example to track service levels in order to help ensure that service level agreements are being kept.

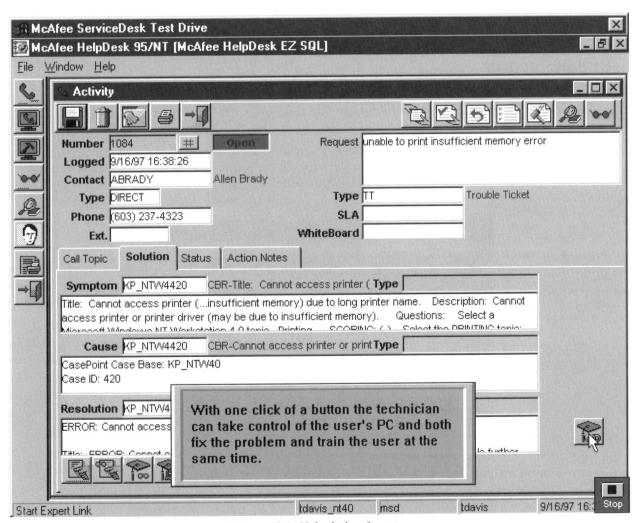

Figure 48.1: Help desk software

> ➢ **Discussion: What other reports would be useful in assessing the efficiency of the help desk service?**

Case study: Call centres

By the year 2001, one in fifty of us will be working in a call centre where hundreds of people take calls on their behalf: the Scottish Highlands, for example, are already dotted with them, including centres for Virgin, the London boroughs and M&G. This 2% of the population will do nothing but answer a telephone all day.

If you have a PC and telephone a number in Watford for technical support, you are quite likely to be rerouted to someone in Dublin, Edinburgh or even Hamburg. The person who answers your call sits in front of a computer, which recommends the questions he asks, and he then searches a database to see if anyone else has ever had the same problem. In other words, your problem is solved by someone who doesn't work for the company you bought your PC from, who wasn't at the number you called, who doesn't even work in the same country, and didn't solve the problem himself!

Source: Tim Phillips, The Guardian 11 December 1997

➤ **Discussion: What are the advantages and disadvantages to an organisation of using a call centre compared with internal help desks using special help desk software?**

Bulletin boards

A bulletin board system (BBS) is an electronic noticeboard to which items of interest, notes, hints and requests for assistance and so on can be pinned. The concept predates wide use of the Internet and some do not require users to subscribe to an Internet Service provider.

A bulletin board can be accessed via a modem in terminal mode, using a program like HyperTerminal in Windows 95. Selecting Start, Programs, Accessories, HyperTerminal brings up a screen which allows you to select New Connection from a File menu. This opens a Connection Description box (Figure 48.2).

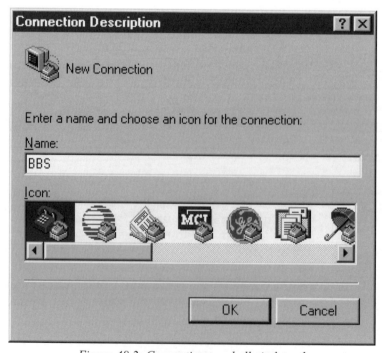

Figure 48.2: Connecting to a bulletin board

After selecting OK and on the next screen, typing in the phone number provided in the software user manual, some user identification and password, a menu of options is displayed and the user can access advice on how to solve their problem.

Various other types of bulletin board serviced by software manufacturers can be accessed via the Internet. These often list 'frequently asked questions' (FAQs) and their answers, as well as providing a forum for users to solve each other's problems or refer them to the software manufacturer's experts.

User booklets

Some software support departments issue new users with an introductory guide to things they might need to know about the product they have purchased. The information given might include:

- Instructions to change the password after logging on for the first time;
- The name and address of their local contact;
- The hours that User Support is open;
- How to get printer paper, toner and other consumables;
- Where to go for training.

Newsletters and support articles

Many software companies produce their own regular newsletters. This typically contains tips on how to get the most out of the software, details of forthcoming support meetings and conferences, FAQs, articles and letters sent in by users describing how they have cleverly solved some obscure problem and previews of the inevitable forthcoming upgrade. Computer magazines also regularly have articles on similar topics.

On-line help

On-line help can be an invaluable aid to anyone learning a new software package. This typically contains an index of topics and a tutorial for beginners. Microsoft Help has a link to a Web site offering various options (Figure 48.3).

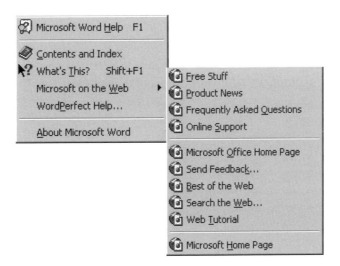

Figure 48.3: On-line help with Internet links

Documentation

Users need different levels of documentation depending on how they are using the software and how expert they are. Clerical workers may need an introductory tutorial, whereas 'knowledge workers' will probably need a reference manual as they use the software for increasingly complex tasks.

➤ **Discussion: What are the relative advantages of on-line help and user manuals?**

Exercises

1. (a) Describe **three** items of information a user support line would log when taking a call from a user. (3)

   (b) Many user support lines need to share problems and potential solutions between a number of operators who are answering calls. Describe **one** method of achieving this. (3)

   (c) Some user support lines also offer a mailbox facility to enable users to log their problems using e-mail. What advantages does this have for
      (i) the software user;
      (ii) the user support staff. (4)

   NEAB IT04 Qu 8 1997

2. Each day a software house logs a large number of calls from its users to its support desk.

   (a) Describe how the support desk might manage these requests to provide an effective service. (3)

   (b) Describe **three** items of information the support desk would require to assist in resolving a user's problem. (3)

   (c) The software house receives complaints from its users that the support desk is providing a poor service. Describe **three** reports that the software house could produce in order to combat the validity of this claim. (6)

   NEAB IT04 Qu 7 Sample paper

3. "As software becomes increasingly easy to use, the need for user support will decline."
   State whether you agree or disagree, giving **two** reasons to support your answer. (4)

   New question

4. Describe briefly **four** features you would expect to find in help desk software designed to be used by a call centre diagnosing users' problems with various software packages. (4)

   New question

Chapter 49 – Training

The need for training

Companies in industrialised countries spend huge amounts of money, often several million pounds a year, on training their employees. There are numerous different reasons why companies perceive training to be a valuable investment.

- Employees need training to give them the skills, attitude and knowledge required to do their jobs safely and well. This is true at all levels in a company, from the new recruit in a supermarket learning how to use the till and interact with customers, to the manager who needs to learn how to motivate the staff and to make effective decisions.

- New employees often need training before they can be reasonably effective within a company. They may need to be trained in the use of hardware or software they have not used before, or on the operational procedures that have to be followed.

- Existing employees require retraining because companies and jobs are constantly changing, new technologies are installed and new procedures are introduced.

- Well-trained employees are likely to be better motivated and have a better chance of promotion on a well-defined career path.

- Training can lead to increased sales, a better service to customers, better quality products, good safety records, and lower staff turnover.

> ➤ **Discussion: Have you worked in an organisation where you were given training? What were the benefits? Have you been in a situation where training was needed but not given?**

Training in the use of information technology

Training staff in the use of new technology is crucial to the success of any computer system. Unless staff at all levels of an organisation know how to use the new technology effectively, investment in a computer system can be a waste of money.

Training for senior managers

Managers who understand fully the benefits and problems associated with the use of information technology are likely to make better decisions than less well-informed colleagues when:

- establishing a corporate information systems strategy;
- appraising advice from ICT professionals either within or outside the organisation;
- allocating resources to information systems.

Training for middle managers

Middle management will be responsible for ensuring that computer systems are correctly used, and that accurate, timely and useful information reaches the right people at the right time. They will also be responsible for the organisation's computer security policy. Therefore, they will need training in how to define information requirements, how to integrate systems and how to realise the potential of a new computer system. They will also need training in the use of software such as spreadsheets, communications software, word processing and specialised software needed for their particular job.

Training for users

When a new software package is introduced into a company, users at different levels of the company may require different levels of training. At the lowest level, for example, a clerical worker may need to know how to load a spreadsheet package, enter the daily or weekly sales figures and print a report. A member of the sales staff in an electrical retailer's may need to know how to enter a customer's details to check their credit rating, and put through a sale. A secretary may need to know how to use a word processor to write and print letters and reports, and how to use function keys to activate macros. These activities are **task-based**.

A middle manager or 'knowledge worker', on the other hand, may need **skill-based** rather than task-based knowledge. A marketing manager who has to give a presentation on the expected sales of a new product may need to use a spreadsheet to analyse and graph actual and projected figures and insert the results into a word processed report for the managing director. An office supervisor may design a style for all internal memos and reports, and create a template and macros to automate certain functions, using a word processing package.

> ➤ **Discussion: A company uses a database package to develop a customer invoicing and information system. Identify the different functions that this system could be used for, and different levels of training that would be required by the people using the package.**

Methods of training

There are several different methods by which users can gain expertise in the use of software packages. These include:

- Computer-based training;
- Watching a video training course;
- Interactive video training;
- On-line tutorials supplied with the software;
- Step-through guides;
- Formal, instructor-led training courses.

Computer-based training

Computer-based training has several benefits.

- For an employer, a major benefit is cost. Training courses can easily cost £500 per day per employee, with accommodation costs as an added extra. The investment in a suitable training package can quickly pay for itself if there are large numbers of employees requiring training.

- Staff can do the training at times which fit in with their workload, causing the least amount of disruption. During a slack period a member of staff can be sent to a training room on the premises to do an hour or two of training, or it may take place at the employee's own computer at their desk.

- Employees can study at their own pace and repeat sections which are difficult or which they have forgotten.

- Standardised training. Instructor-led training varies with the trainer and the training centre, whereas computer-aided training offers standardisation. However it cannot guarantee that all employees will gain the same benefit; it is very easy to keep pressing the 'Next' button without taking anything in!

> ➤ **Discussion: Have you ever used an on-line tutorial or other form of computer-based tutorial? What are the disadvantages of this method of learning?**

Instructor-led courses

For some, nothing can replace a good instructor. As one trainer said, "We are not very keen on computer-assisted learning because it is too impersonal. The best training results from the personal inspiration of a good trainer, from his or her ability to communicate with the trainee and whet the appetite for further knowledge and the ways to use that knowledge to good effect." Other advantages of classroom learning include the following:

- Learning is essentially a communal activity and students learn a lot from debate and discussion in the class.

- Peer collaboration in learning can help to develop general problem-solving skills. Learning together has the potential to produce gains superior to learning alone.

- Individuals often have a valuable store of personal knowledge which they can share with a group.

- Many jobs involve working together in teams and rely on successful collaboration with colleagues: formal education in a classroom can help prepare people to work together in groups.

Skills updating

Employees do not need training only when they start a new job, or when new technology is introduced; there is an ongoing need for skills updating and refreshing. An initial training course may be given in the rudiments of the software, which employees need to practice before they can take in new information. Some functions may not be introduced initially; for example year-end procedures may not be taught to everyone, but extra training may be needed for those who need to use these functions. As the new system becomes better understood, managers may want to learn new skills using advanced features. Employees who have been or are about to be promoted may need to learn new aspects of an information system.

Corporate training strategy

Companies with a commitment to training generally have well thought out objectives in their training programmes, and a clear idea of the benefits of training. The primary goal of training in one large company, for example, is stated as "to produce outstanding quality and service, to achieve total customer satisfaction, aggressive sales growth and optimum profits."

Without a training policy, companies can quickly lose their competitive edge. Experience shows that an unable, unwilling unresponsive or unskilled workforce can undermine or negate even the best strategies. On the other hand, companies which are managing the development of their people show enhanced performance because the employees are able, consistent, co-operative, responsible and solvers of problems.

The Department of Trade and Industry has published a booklet entitled 'Partnerships with People' which suggests ideas for a corporate training strategy. (Figure 49.1.)

Ideas worth trying

Develop appraisal systems which focus on individual development. Look at other jobs in the organisation that an individual may aspire to, encourage the development of necessary attributes to take them on.

Seek advice from the TEC/LEC or specialist training adviser to design a development programme for managers.

Provide business training for supervisors, technical managers, union representatives.

Investigate NVQs and encourage staff to take relevant qualifications.

Encourage key staff to develop training skills so they can pass on knowledge.

Make booklets and other self-help learning packages available to staff.

Develop links with local FE colleges – reimburse college fees in full or in part, to encourage people to get into the learning habit.

Encourage relevant people to take HND, degree or professional qualifications.

(Partnerships with People – a DTI booklet)

Figure 49.1: Points to consider in a corporate training strategy

Exercises

1. You are asked to advise an organisation on the introduction of a new software package.
    (a) With the aid of **three** examples, explain why different users may require different levels of training. (6)
    (b) Following the initial training you advise subsequent training for users. Give **two** reasons why this may be required, other than financial gain for the agency. (4)
    NEAB IT04 Qu 9 1997

2. Describe briefly **five** facilities you would expect to find in an on-line tutorial for a spreadsheet package. (5)
    New question

3. Why should a corporation have a training strategy for staff? (3)
    Give **three** points that could be included in such a strategy. (3)
    New question

4. Describe, with the aid of examples, **three** different methods of providing training in the use of software, and justify their use. (9)
    AQA ICT4 Qu 5 January 2003

Chapter 50 – Project Management

Introduction

A **project** is a short-term activity bringing together people with different skills, equipment and resources to achieve specified objectives. Project management often begins with the selection of a project manager and a project team. The project itself must be broken down into tasks, whose sequence and estimated time for completion is calculated and documented. Projects usually have the following characteristics:

- They have a specific objective – for example, the networking of all the computers in a college, or the introduction of a new computerised enrolment system;
- They must be developed within a specified time period;
- They must be developed within a given budget;
- A team of people is brought together temporarily from different areas to work on the project. When the project is finished, the team will be disbanded.

Selection of a project manager

Once a project has been given the go-ahead by senior management, the first step is the appointment of a project manager. The project manager needs to have the necessary technical skills, but just as important are the managerial skills needed to be able to lead and motivate a group of people from different departments and different levels within the organisation. Good interpersonal skills and business experience are also essential assets.

The tasks of a project manager

The project manager must:
- Plan and staff the project;
- Analyse risk;
- Monitor progress;
- Adjust schedules;
- Report project status;
- Control budgets and salaries;
- Prepare performance appraisals;
- Interact with users, corporate management and project personnel.

Courses in project management are offered by many educational and training establishments.

The project team

One of the first tasks of the project manager may be to pick the project development team. Studies have shown that an ideal team size is between 5 and 7 members, and that as the team size increases, level of job satisfaction drops, absenteeism and turnover rise, and the project may start to miss deadlines. Some projects, of course, are far too large and complex to have such a small team.

> ➤ **Discussion: Adding more people to a team which is behind schedule often has the effect of putting it even further behind schedule. Why?**

Regardless of the size of the project team, it should have a balance of theoreticians and practitioners, idealists and realists, technical and business specialists. Boehm in his book Software Engineering Economics (Prentice Hall 1981) listed five principles of software staffing:

1. **Principle of top talent**. Employ fewer but better people.

2. **Principle of job matching**. Match skills and motivations available to the task at hand.

3. **Principle of team balance**. There needs to be a balance between the technical skills, knowledge and personality characteristics of team members.

4. **Principle of phase out**. There will inevitably be a misfit on the team resulting in "unhealthy results in the long run". Getting the misfit out may not be easy but must be done with adequate thought, time and sympathy.

5. **Principle of career progression**. Bring out the best in people by enabling them to work on tasks that will help them to progress.

Project planning and scheduling

The project manager will divide up the project into phases and the phases into tasks. This may be done by identifying *milestones* which represent significant progress towards completion. Next, the skills that are needed for each of these tasks are identified and the time required for completion of each task calculated, based on the skills and availability of staff. A team leader may be appointed for each of these tasks, and the cost of completion of each task calculated.

Task definition forms the basis of the overall project plan, on which schedules and budgets are based. It is also used to track the progress of a project. Overlooking tasks is a common cause of cost and time overruns in projects, so it is very important to define all the tasks that need to be completed. Tasks that are commonly overlooked include training (or learning new skills), production of reports, project reviews, correction of errors and omissions.

Example: It is proposed to install a new computer network in the 6th form block of a school. What are the tasks involved in completing this project?

Tasks:

1. Carry out initial feasibility study

2. Invite tenders from suppliers

3. Choose a supplier

4. Purchase computers

5. Recable the building

6. Draw up plans for new classroom layout

7. Convert classroom

8. Install computers

9. Purchase network software

10. Install hardware and network software

11. Test network

12. Install end-user software

> ➢ **Discussion: Is this list complete? Can any of the tasks be carried out simultaneously?**

Many project managers keep a day-by-day log of the progress and difficulties encountered in a project, which can be an invaluable aid to planning the project schedule of future projects.

Project reviews

Most project schedules need constant updating and revision during the course of the project. It is important to have a formal *review process* to monitor and control the progress of a project. Review sessions every few weeks or so may be held in order to:

- Compare progress against the project schedule;

- Keep management informed and involved in the progress of the project;

- Reconfirm that current task lists and schedules are correct and on target;

- Identify any problems or slippage and come up with solutions;

- Encourage team spirit and communication between team members.

In spite of regular reviews and reports, many projects fail to meet deadlines and cost considerably over budget. Some projects may be so innovative that it is difficult to make accurate estimates. Sometimes excessive pressure on team members to keep to deadlines makes them hesitant to report problems, and sometimes the requirements of the project are changed in midstream. The larger and more complex the project, the more room there is for error. Louis Fried, a project manager, had a number of rules for project management including one which read "Any task that requires more than 10 people can't be done". ("The Rules of Project Management", *Journal of Information Systems Management Summer 1992*)

Characteristics of a good team

A good team requires:

- leadership – someone who can inspire and keep the team motivated, and who understands exactly what has to be achieved;

- appropriate allocation of tasks – the best person for the particular job;

- adherence to standards – proper procedures carried out, documentation kept up to date, etc;

- monitoring, costing, controlling – progress must be monitored, schedules adjusted, costs kept within agreed limits and not allowed to spiral out of control.

Exercises

1. A project team has been appointed by a firm of consultants to write a tailor-made customer billing and accounts system for a medium-sized business. The project team consists of a project leader (the systems analyst), two programmers and a technician. The project is falling behind schedule and the managing director of the company decides to allocate two more programmers to the team. The project continues to fall further behind.

    Give **three** reasons why this might be so. (6)

    New question

2. The management of a college decides that a college-wide network should be installed to link together all the computers in the college. The estimated cost of the project is £1 million. What factors should the project manager take into account when planning the estimated time to completion of the project? (6)

    New question

3. A firm is creating a team to plan, design and implement an IT project. Describe **four** characteristics of a good IT project team. (8)

    NEAB IT04 Qu 7 1998

Chapter 51 – Codes of Practice

Ethics and computing

Ethics is the science of morals; the study of ethics is the study of how to make choices between right and wrong. Why should we care about ethics? The number of ethical decisions of one kind or another that we face in our personal and professional lives makes it imperative that we care. Some unethical decisions may be illegal; others may have drastic consequences for our lives or careers. Therefore, each of us must care about ethics as a matter of self-interest. In addition, we are all members of society, and ethical decision-making is vital to creating the sort of world in which we want to live.

> ➤ **Discussion: Is 'computer ethics' any different from other kinds of ethics? Is there a difference between**
>
>   **– browsing through files on someone's PC, and rummaging through their locker?**
>
>   **– sending obscene messages over a computer network, and writing anonymous obscene notes on paper to someone?**
>
>   **– using unlicensed software and travelling on a train without paying?**

Factors in ethical decision-making

Ethical decisions, whether or not they involve information technology, are rarely straightforward. There is often not a straight choice between right and wrong – rather, the choice lies between the lesser of two evils. Of course, it is wrong to lie, cheat or steal – but is it wrong to steal food if your child is starving, lie to a friend about how good they look, give a fellow student a helping hand by writing most of his program or essay for him? A poor decision can have a number of undesirable consequences. People may be left hurt or offended, employee morale may be adversely affected, customers may be lost, a company may go bankrupt.

Sometimes the law prescribes whether a certain action is legal. Often an ethical principle is the basis of the Law; for example, the recognition that an individual has the right to ownership of an original work has led to copyright laws being enacted. In other cases, the law does not provide an answer and it is then useful to have a set of guidelines for how to act.

Formal guidelines in the computing industry

When a person accepts employment in any company, he or she accepts moral responsibilities that define appropriate behaviour in that job – responsibilities referred to as professional ethics. Two factors apply to all professionals and influence their actions: professional relationships and professional efficacy ('doing a good job'). Most professions have ethical codes or standards that explain appropriate professional behaviour and efficacious behaviour in various situations, and the computing profession is no exception. Various professional bodies such as the British Computer Society (BCS) and the Association for Computing Machinery (ACM) produce their own Code of Ethics and Professional Conduct. (You can look up the BCS Code of Conduct on the Internet, using the web address www.bcs.org.uk, and then searching for Code of Conduct using the index.

The ACM Code of Conduct is shown below:

ACM Code of Ethics

ACM* Code of Ethics and Professional Conduct

1. GENERAL MORAL IMPERATIVES
As an ACM member I will ..

1.1	Contribute to society and human well-being
1.2	Avoid harm to others
1.3	Be honest and trustworthy
1.4	Be fair and take action not to discriminate
1.5	Honour property rights including copyrights and patents
1.6	Give proper credit for intellectual property
1.7	Respect the privacy of others
1.8	Honour confidentiality

2. MORE SPECIFIC PROFESSIONAL RESPONSIBILITIES
As an ACM computing professional I will ..

2.1	Strive to achieve the highest quality, effectiveness and dignity in both the process and products of professional work
2.2	Acquire and maintain professional competence
2.3	Know and respect existing laws pertaining to professional work
2.4	Accept and provide appropriate professional review
2.5	Give comprehensive and thorough evaluations of computer systems and their impacts, including analysis of possible risks
2.6	Honour contracts, agreements, and assigned responsibilities
2.7	Improve public understanding of computing and its consequences
2.8	Access computing and communication resources only when authorised to do so

3. ORGANIZATION LEADERSHIP IMPERATIVES
As an ACM member and an organisational leader I will ..

3.1	Articulate social responsibilities of members of an organisational unit and encourage full acceptance of those responsibilities
3.2	Manage personnel and resources to design and build information systems that enhance the quality of working life
3.3	Acknowledge and support proper and authorised uses of an organisation's computing and communications resources
3.4	Ensure that users and those who will be affected by a system have their needs clearly articulated during the assessment and design of requirements. Later the system must be validated to meet user requirements.
3.5	Articulate and support policies that protect the dignity of users and others affected by a computing system
3.6	Create opportunities for members of the organisation to learn the principles and limitations of computer systems

4. COMPLIANCE WITH THE CODE
As an ACM member I will ..

4.1	Uphold and promote the principles of this Code
4.2	Treat violations of this Code as inconsistent with membership of the ACM

Figure 51.1: The ACM Code of Ethics and Professional Conduct

Codes of practice

The ACM code of Ethics and Professional Conduct above lays out a general code of practice for ICT professionals. Here is a summary of some of the main points:

1. **Contribute to society and human well-being**. Share your expert knowledge freely with others, and be prepared to help colleagues and others when needed.

2. **Avoid harm to others**. This could include passing on a virus through carelessness or not following company procedures.

3. **Be honest and trustworthy**.

4. **Honour property rights including copyrights and patents**.

5. **Give proper credit for intellectual property**. Do not try and pass off another person's work as your own.

6. **Respect the privacy of others**. For example, if you have authorised access to confidential files of information, do not 'gossip' about this information, or pass on other people's personal information. Do not read other people's e-mail.

Employee code of conduct

An employee code of conduct can be an effective measure against computer misuse and abuse. Potential employees need to be checked out carefully before they are hired and, once hired, required to sign an employment contract which sets out the types of misconduct, including computer abuse, which will result in dismissal without notice.

Once new employees actually join, they should be given training which includes a general awareness of computer crime and misuse, the company's policy on security, the use of illegal software, the introduction of viruses, reading other people's e-mail and privacy issues including the Data Protection Act. They should be instructed to change their password frequently and to refer to the company's security manual from time to time. Their responsibilities and authorisation for specific duties should be clearly specified.

> ➤ **Discussion: What sort of 'rules' would you expect to find in an employee code of conduct? Draw up a 'code of conduct' for students using school or college computers.**

Using informal guidelines to make ethical decisions

Informal guidelines can be useful in reaching an ethical decision. Here are some long-standing, broad-based ethical principles to help decide between conflicting demands:

- **The Golden Rule.** Do unto others as you would have them do unto you. Think about the effects of your actions, and put yourself in the position of someone who would be affected.

- **The Greatest Good/Least Harm.** When choosing between courses of action, choose the one which achieves the greatest good for the greatest number of people, and causes the least harm.

- **Kant's Categorical Imperative**. If the action is not right for everyone to take, then it's not right for anyone to take. Think about what would happen if everyone acted as you propose to do.

- **The Slippery Slope Rule**. Actions that bring about a small, acceptable change but that, if taken repeatedly, would lead to unacceptable changes, should not be taken in the first place.

Case study 1

Staff working for a large company called Cyber Electronics frequently complain of various faults on their PCs. Printers that fail to print, software that won't load, files going missing and dollar signs appearing instead of pound signs are among countless faults commonly reported.

Until recently Ben, the software support analyst, was difficult to track down as he was always roaming from room to room, building to building, fixing problems of one sort or another. Recently, however, the company has invested in a software package called ScreenScape which enables the computer support staff to view anyone's screen from their own PC. Ben is now able to spend almost all of his time at his desk, taking calls from users, calling up their screens and advising the user what to do or fixing the problem himself. Users are delighted with the improved service.

One day he happens to mention the improvement to a Senior Manager in the Accounts Department, who is instantly interested. He asks "You mean you can see exactly what any member of staff is doing on his PC at any time?" "That's right", replies Ben. "Well, I'd like a copy of that software installed on my PC. Can you fix that for me? I have a suspicion that one of my staff is involved in something illegal which could be potentially disastrous for this company, but I've never been able to catch her at it. This could be very useful."

Ben is taken aback. "I'm not sure I can do that. I'll have to let you know."

➢ **What is the ethical dilemma facing Ben? Should he supply the software to the Senior Manager? What are the conflicting issues here?**

Case study 2

Programs which can read and sift 10 CVs in less than a minute and a half are increasingly replacing humans as the first screening stage in the recruitment process, particularly for big companies which receive hundreds of CVs each week. If you've recently applied for a job with Cable and Wireless, Mercury, ICL or Sainsbury's, chances are it was a computer which determined whether you advanced to the next round in the job hunt.

The simplest programs work by searching for key words, so if the job requires knowledge of a particular software package, the computer will pick out applications which mention this word.

➢ **What are the advantages and disadvantages to the employer, and the prospective employee, of using a computer to sift applications? Do you think this is an ethical procedure? Justify your answer.**

Case study 3

Times are bad at B.G. Computer Consultants, with some employees facing redundancy and others who have already been made redundant. Only last week Tom was given 15 minutes to clear his desk before being escorted from the building and his User ID and password removed from the company network. Helen and Ian are fairly confident, however, that their jobs as systems analysts are secure, since they are both working on large contracts. Ian in fact is on the verge of taking out a huge mortgage on a new house. He has often told Helen that if the company ever 'did the dirty on him' as he put it, he would get his own back in no uncertain terms.

One day Helen is working on a presentation. The figures she needs are in a file on the boss's computer, and he is out to lunch. She happens to know his password (unbeknownst to him) and decides to look for the file. Purely accidentally she comes across a memo indicating that Ian is to be made redundant as soon as the contract is completed.

> **Should Helen warn Ian about his forthcoming redundancy before he commits himself to a mortgage that he won't be able to afford? Who benefits? Who is harmed?**

> **What changes to company policies are needed to prevent such a situation arising in the future?**

Exercises

1. Use the Internet to look up the British Computer Society's Code of Practice. Describe briefly **four** general areas that you would expect such a Code of Practice to cover. (8)

   New question

2. Describe briefly a situation within an Information Technology environment which could pose a moral or ethical dilemma. Describe briefly **three** informal rules which could help in reaching an ethical decision in how to deal with the situation. (5)

   New question

3. As the IT manager for a large company, you have been asked to develop an employee code of conduct. Describe four issues which might be included in such a code. (8)

   NEAB IT05 Qu 4 1998

4. New employees joining a company are each asked to sign an agreement to adhere to a code of practice for using the organisation's computer system.

   Explain **four** issues that such a code of practice should address. (8)

   AQA ICT4 Qu 3 June 2002

ICT4 – Sample Questions and Answers

1. (a) What is meant by a Management Information System? (4)

   (b) State **four** factors which could contribute to the success or failure of a Management Information System. (4)

   NEAB IT04 Qu 3 1998

Notes:

Unless you have memorised answers from the textbook (always dangerous) to questions such as this one, it helps to have an example of a MIS in mind, if possible from your own experience, or one that you have studied. For revision purposes, you should always try and write down an answer before consulting the textbook or looking at the suggested answer. Then at least you know what you don't know.

OK, so a MIS is a system which provides information to management (0 marks so far). Try carrying on… in order to help them do what? What sort of managers – managing directors, or shop floor managers? Where does the data come from that is turned into useful information? What form does this information take? A string of numbers, or a bar chart?

The answers to part (b) are very clearly laid out in Chapter 37 and are summarised in the AQA Specification for ICT4. You would be well advised to read very carefully through the specification and use it as basis for revision.

Suggested Answer:

(a) A Management Information System is a system to convert data from internal and external sources into information in an appropriate format. The information produced will be used by managers at different levels of an organisation to help them to plan, control and make effective decisions.

(b) Any of the following can lead to the failure of a MIS:

Inadequate analysis – the problems and exact needs of managers are not fully understood when the system is designed.

Excessive management demands – managers sometimes ask for information which is hard to extract from the system and which they do not in the end even need.

Lack of teamwork – a good team requires a good leader, and the ICT manager must lead, motivate and control his team effectively, and also take on board the whole company's requirements.

Lack of professional standards – systems must be developed using agreed standards for each stage from analysis to the final user documentation. Poorly documented systems are difficult to amend and maintain. Users need clear documentation so that they know exactly what to do.

2. Information systems are capable of producing strategic and operational information. With the aid of examples, explain the difference between these two levels of information, clearly stating the level of personnel involved in using each one. (6)

   NEAB IT04 Qu 3 1999

Notes:

Here you have to alternately imagine yourself as the managing director of a company, producing anything from cars to hamburgers, and one of the workers engaged in, say, chasing up customers who have not paid for goods received. What sort of information would you need in each case?

Suggested answer:

Strategic information is used to inform senior managers at Board level to assist in planning or budgeting, or deciding in which direction the company should expand. For example statistics on the success of a new online shopping facility may be important in deciding whether to expand that side of the business. Operational level information is used by middle management or clerical workers to assist in daily tasks such as 'When was the order dispatched to Henry VII school?' or 'How many customers have debts of over £250 outstanding over more than 30 days?'

---

3. A particular organisation is upgrading its computer-based stock control system. The previous data collection system was OMR based.

    One function of the system is to allow stock levels to be monitored on a regular basis.

    (a) State **three** other alternative methods of collecting stock control data. (3)

    (b) What factors, other than cost, will determine the method of data collection? (4)

    (c) The software used to control the system must support an audit trail. Explain what is meant by the term 'audit trail', and state why this functionality is necessary. (6)

    NEAB IT04 Qu 5 1999

Notes:

You have to be very clear in your mind what sort of stock control system is being described here. For example if you are selling books in a bookshop, the quantity in stock is automatically adjusted every time you sell a book so there would be no need to monitor stock regularly by actually counting what was on the shelves. However if you are selling meals in a restaurant, you might very well want to check stocks of basic items on a daily or weekly basis. How will this be done? In this question, I think you can assume that you are to describe methods *either* of collecting data about stock that is actually physically counted on the shelves of the stockroom or warehouse, *or* through sales at the till or invoicing system.

Parts (b) and (c) are fairly standard questions with fairly standard answers. The main thing to understand about audit trails is that they provide a means of checking all the transactions that have been processed. You can't have a system which simply tells you that you have 4,168 mobile phones in stock but does not explain how this figure is arrived at when you started 3 months ago with 10,000 being delivered.

Suggested answer:

(a) Stock control data may be collected at the tills with a bar code reader by scanning each item as it is sold. The stock level will be automatically adjusted by the system.
Alternatively the stock on the shelves may be barcoded and using a hand-held laser gun the bar codes can be read and the data transferred later electronically to the main computer system.
Data at a till may be collected using a special 'touch till' where, for example, the staff touch a symbol for each drink or food item ordered in a restaurant. The stock information will then be automatically updated.

(b) Factors which determine the method of data collection include:
   * The volume of stock and the number of transactions performed daily;
   * The need to have completely up-to-date information on stock levels;

- The diversity of stock. Not everything can be bar-coded, for example portions of vegetables.

(c) An audit trail provides a means of tracking every transaction that has been entered into the system so that it is possible to see how a particular figure was arrived at. It is possible to get a printout of all transactions which affect one particular line of stock, for example. Some systems record who has used the system, when and for how long, which enables any unauthorised or suspicious use to be monitored.

It is essential to maintain an audit trail in order to meet legal requirements to do so, as every business must produce a set of accounts based on verifiable facts. Also, an audit trail is a protection against fraud and against theft of stock.

---

4. A multi-site college is considering the introduction of an IT based system to log visitors. The current system is based on a manual log at reception. The new system will capture visual images of visitors together with details of their visit. The introduction of this system will cause considerable change for staff and visitors.

In the context of this example describe **four** factors that the management should consider when introducing this change. (8)

NEAB IT05 Qu 4 1998

Notes:

The key word here is *change* which if you have done your revision should set bells ringing and remind you to look again at the topic 'The Management of Change' (Chapter 44). However failing that, use some imagination and common sense. You can think of some aspects that will affect visitors and some that will affect staff at various levels. (This system seems pretty pointless to me, how is the management going to convince lecturers who have no money for textbooks that it is worth the expense? Will some anarchic Computing lecturer smash the camera at the end of his evening session?)

Suggested answer:

The management should consider how the change will affect the staff at reception and whether they will object to the change. Their support should be gained by explaining the benefits of the new system and involving them in planning details. Training for staff to operate the new system will be required. It is possible that some visitors may object to having their photographs taken, and this needs to be investigated. The management should also consider whether such a plan is cost-effective and whether the information captured by the new system will actually be used by anyone. Involvement of those who are likely to use the information is essential to determine their requirements and to gain their support. Ideas and misgivings should be listened to and taken into consideration when planning the system.

---

5. The Head of a school decides to adopt an IT package to maintain pupils' records of attainment. The package will be used throughout the school.
   (a) (i)   Identify three potential users of this package. (3)
       (ii) With the aid of examples, describe the different types of documentation that each user will require. (6)
   (b) Training in the use of this package may be provided by a variety of methods other than formal training courses. Describe **two** possible alternative methods. (4)

NEAB IT04 Qu 5 1998

Notes:

Note that the potential *users of the IT package* will be within the school, even though the documents produced may be bound in a folder and used by a potential employer. So confine your answers to users within the school. Part (a) (ii) is at first sight open to misinterpretation – does it mean the documentation that would be needed to use the system, for example to input data or customise reports, or the output that would be produced by the system in the form of reports? Just be sure you know which you are talking about.

Suggested answer:

(a) The package will be used by the **Form Tutor** to enter data regarding individual pupils' progress and levels of attainment. User documentation would be required to show a teacher how to log on to the system, input student data and print out reports for each student or for a whole class.

Management would use the system to produce school statistics on achievement for the school prospectus etc. The results might of course be produced by the **clerical support staff** using the system rather than the Head Teacher. The documentation required would be advice on how to perform queries, sorts, etc to produce the required statistics.

Technical Support Staff would be required to customise reports, install the system on new computers, respond to error messages, perform backups etc. They would need technical documentation on how to perform these functions.

(b) Training could be provided by:

An on-line tutorial so that the user can sit at the computer they are actually going to use and go through the steps to input data, select reports etc;

A video which has a tutor explaining how to perform all the tasks, the advantage being that the video can be watched anywhere, even at home at the end of an exhausting day coping with Year 10;

A step-by-step user guide can be used by following it through while trying out each step on a computer;

(Could also mention: One person can go for formal training and then show relevant parts of the system to smaller groups or individuals on an informal basis.)

---

6. A software house has a user support department that provides a range of services to customers including telephone advice and the supply of data fixes for corrupt files. The department uses a computer-based logging system to store details of incoming telephone calls from users (a call management system). The system is capable of producing a variety of reports via a report generator.

   (a) The software house receives complaints from its users that this department is providing a poor service. Describe three reports that the software house could produce to examine the validity of this claim. (6)

   (b) The department uses traditional mail to receive disks containing corrupt files and to return them with the data fixed. However, the department now wishes to use electronic communications based on ISDN. Describe **two** potential advantages and **one** potential disadvantage to the customer of this proposed change. (6)

NEAB IT04 Qu 7 1999

Notes:

Think what would constitute a poor service. Not being there to answer the call, taking too long to answer, not being able to fix the problem, etc. This should give you some ideas for reports that could monitor these events. Be aware that you will get *one* mark for writing, for example, 'a report which logs the response time to a customer call'. For the second mark, you will have to give more detail.

In part (b) avoid answers such as quicker, cheaper, more convenient unless you can fully justify your answer. You will get no marks for suggesting that the user may not be connected to the Internet, because for heaven's sake, they should be! And no marks for suggesting they will save the cost of a stamp by not having to post a disk.

Suggested answer:

(a) One problem with help lines from software houses is that they are often inundated with calls at busy periods of the day and the user is held in a queue, for periods of up to half an hour or more. A report which logs the number of calls taken per hour, and the actual response time until the user gets to speak to a member of the user support staff, will show whether waiting times are acceptable.

When a user calls they are usually asked for their software serial number and the nature of their problem. The time spent on the phone explaining how to solve the problem is also logged. Therefore a report analysing the amount of time solving each different type of problem, and which member of staff fielded the call, would show whether there was consistency in the amount of time spent by different staff members on solving similar types of problem.

A third report might show the number of problems that could not be resolved by the staff at the help desk, or which had to be passed to someone else to solve, and compare this figure to the number of problems that were solved satisfactorily the first time.

(b) Advantages to customer: Many data files are too large to fit on a floppy disk and zip disks are expensive, and not all users will have a zip drive, so it is impractical to copy large data files to disk.

It would be possible for a user at the Help desk to take over the user's screen remotely, calling it up on their own screen to solve the problem or provide the fix immediately.

A disadvantage could be that the service could be more expensive, and the client would also have to bear the cost of an ISDN line.

---

7. A company has three departments to handle finance, buildings and equipment maintenance. Each department currently operates a separate IT system. The company wishes to improve the efficiency of the operations by implementing a common corporate system across all three departments. In order to achieve this improvement, the company has decided to select members of staff from each department to form a project team to plan, design and implement the new system.

   (a) Describe three corporate level factors the team should consider when planning the new system.
   (6)

   (b) At their first meeting the team decide to sub-divide the project into a series of tasks. Describe **two** advantages of this approach.
   (4)
   NEAB IT05 Qu 8 1999

Notes:

Remember the factors that affect the success or failure of a Management Information System? Time to dust them off again. Also, the new system implies *change*, so the implications of change could form part of your answer.

In part (b), you should be able to call on your own experience of group assignments, but you must make sure you relate them to an ICT project.

Suggested answer:

(a) It is essential that the management from each department is involved in the planning stages to ensure that the new system meets their requirements and will have their support. Employees at all levels of the organisation are likely to be affected by the new system and they should also be informed and their views taken into account. A proper training program will have to be worked out for both operations staff and management. The implications of the change on employment conditions and practices need to be considered. It is possible that some jobs may disappear or that staff may need to be redeployed when the new system becomes operational.

(b) All ICT projects of this nature will break down into various phases such as Analysis, Design, Implementation etc. Within these phases there will be subtasks such as designing the user interface, writing programs, writing user documentation etc. By breaking down the project into subtasks each member of the team can be allocated tasks that play to their strengths – one may be a good analyst and communicator, one a good programmer etc. A project that consists of a number of clearly defined tasks is very much easier to control as it is clear when one task such as 'Set up the database table' has been completed. It also means that if someone leaves the team before the project is completed, their tasks can more easily be re-allocated as it is clear what needs to be done and what sort of person is needed, e.g. a good technical person or someone who has a good understanding of the business etc.

---

8. Organisations and IT professionals are required to comply with a legal framework when introducing and using IT systems. In addition there will normally be a code of practice.

    (a) Define what is meant by a 'code of practice'. (2)

    (b) Describe **two** ways in which institutions, such as the British Computer Society, promote professionalism for individuals within the IT industry. (2)

    NEAB IT01 Qu 5 1998

Notes:

No getting away from it, you probably need to have attended the lecture on this one or at least read through Chapter 51 if you were unable to drag yourself out of bed on the day.

Suggested answer:

(a) A code of practice lays out the general 'rules' that an ICT professional should follow, though it does not have the force of law. It will lay down the standard of behaviour and actions expected of an employee within an organisation. For example, employees may be forbidden by the code of practice to send e-mails containing inflammatory / derogatory material or jokes in questionable taste.

(b) The BCS has its own code of ethics which members are expected to abide by. Membership is by examination or professional status within the industry. It also holds seminars, meetings and lectures which enable professionals to get together, exchange ideas and learn from each other.

---

9. "Information systems are mission critical, the consequences of failure could prove disastrous." Discuss this statement, including in your discussion:

    • the potential threats to the system

    • the concept of risk analysis

    • the corporate consequences of system failure

    • the factors which should be considered when designing the 'contingency plan' to enable a recovery from disaster. (20)

    Quality of language will be assessed in this question

    NEAB IT04 Qu 9 1998

Notes:

There will be 4 marks allocated to each of the bullet points and 4 marks for 'quality of language'. (See the advice for question 9 at the end of IT01 for more detail on how marks are allocated for this, and also advice on how to construct your essay.)

Try to make 2 or 3 good points for each part of the question and then *discuss* these points. You will not get 4 marks for simply listing 4 potential threats to a system – you'll get 2 marks if you're lucky. The intelligent, analytical discussion is an essential ingredient of the essay question, which is why it is a good discriminator between strong and weak candidates. But at least if you know what is expected you can give it your best shot!

Suggested answer:

One potential threat to a system is the occurrence of a 'natural' disaster such as a fire, flood or earthquake. The likelihood of earthquakes or hurricanes may be low in some areas but every organisation must make provision for the physical destruction of its hardware, software or data. Hardware failure such as a hard disk crash could destroy vital data in a fraction of a second.

A second threat to an information system is the corruption of data, whether accidentally or deliberately. This could happen because it has been infected by a virus, because an operator has followed the wrong procedure when inputting data, or because of a program error. A disgruntled employee could deliberately cause data to be corrupted by hacking into a database and altering or deleting data, for example.

Risk analysis is the process of weighing up the threats to the computer system and the likely consequences of data loss against the cost of protecting the system. First of all the possible threats to information systems within the company must be established. There may be many information systems and some may be more at risk than others, and some may be more 'mission-critical' than others. It may be a disaster for an online system to be out of action for more than an hour or two – for example on a Stock Exchange or a computerised Ambulance information system, or even the EPOS system at a supermarket. On the other hand some systems such as a mail order invoicing system may not be critically affected if it is out of action for a day, but it is crucial that data is not lost.

Most businesses will not survive the loss of their data files. The loss of customer records, supplier records, accounts and stock control records would make it difficult to continue in business. Surveys show that a significant number of businesses collapse within a short time of a significant data loss. Moreover, the directors of a company may be prosecuted by the Health and Safety Executive if loss of essential business data or safety data adversely affects the health and safety of the public (for example, by losing medical records) or the environment. Under the Data Protection Act, companies have a legal obligation to keep data safe and secure.

When designing a contingency plan to enable recovery from disaster, key elements will include

- A list of the most critical business functions;

- A list of the facilities, hardware, software, data, personnel and other equipment that are necessary to support those functions;

- A method for securing access to all necessary resources;

- A method for getting in touch with all key personnel;

- A step-by-step course of action to follow to implement the plan;

- Education and training of personnel involved in implementing the plan;

- Regular drills to test the effectiveness of the plan.

---

10. A large chain of supermarkets makes use of data processing systems and information systems.
    (a) With the aid of suitable examples, identify the difference between a *data processing system* and an *information system*. (4)
    (b) Describe, with an example of each, the role of an information system in decision making for the following levels of supermarket management:
        (i) tactical;
        (ii) Strategic. (4)
    (c) Give an example of how a data processing operation in a supermarket might provide data for a company-wide information system. (2)

AQA ICT4 Qu 8 June 2002

Notes:

Part (a) is straightforward if you recall that a data processing system records and processes the day-by-day transactions or events that take place, and an information system is used by managers planning and making decisions. Give examples that are relevant to the supermarket.

In part (b), you need to understand the difference between *tactics* and *strategy*. The same words can be used in many situations – the *tactics* in a particular football match might be to keep passing to the very strong player in mid-field, but the overall *strategy* of the club may be to sell the very expensive players and build a team with young, promising talent. Strategy involves a higher level of decision-making than tactics, and has more far-reaching consequences.

Part (c) is a bit ambiguous, so read the question several times very carefully. What is it getting at? Is the question asking how the data collected might be useful to the whole company? Or is it asking exactly how the data might be communicated to the whole company, e.g. by a wide area network? The whole unit is about data and information which probably gives you a clue.

Suggested answer:

(a) A data processing system involves the input, storing and processing of regularly occurring transactions. For example every time an item is sold a transaction occurs, and this is input to the computer system by scanning the item's bar code. The processing that takes place might be to reduce the quantity in stock by one. The output could be a till receipt.

An information system is typically a database which will be used by management to help them monitor and control the running of the supermarket. An example of information could be how much money has been taken on each till every day over a one month period. This could be compared with the same period one year ago, or one month ago.

(b) (i) Tactical information is used to improve the day-by-day operation of the supermarket. The information on how much money is taken at each till might be used to make a decision on whether certain employees should be rewarded for excellent performance, whether others needed further training, or whether some tills needed to be relocated.

(ii) Strategic information is used by top-level management to plan the strategy for the next few years. For example if the amount taken at each till has been steadily increasing month on month, the management may decide to open a new store or extend the existing one.

(c) The data processing system which records all sales at the tills may be used to provide information on which new items are particularly popular. Other stores in the company may then decide to stock them.

Section 5

Information: Policy, Strategy and Systems

In this section:

Chapter 52 –   *Policy and Strategy*

Chapter 53 –   *Security and Backup Policies*

Chapter 54 –   *Software Evaluation*

Chapter 55 –   *Data Modelling*

Chapter 56 –   *Relational Database Design*

Chapter 57 –   *Database Management*

Chapter 58 –   *Communication and Information Systems*

Chapter 59 –   *Network Security and Accounting*

Chapter 60 –   *Data Communications and Standards*

Chapter 61 –   *Human-Computer Interaction*

Chapter 62 –   *Software Acquisition and Testing*

Sample Questions and Answers

Chapter 52 – Policy and Strategy

The challenge of information management

Within the space of a few decades, businesses have moved from having one mainframe computer to process data for payroll, stock control and customer accounts to having company-wide, often worldwide networks of computers affecting and controlling every aspect of their business. Computers are no longer a centralised resource operated and understood by a few knowledgeable experts: at every level of a company, employees will be interacting with and using computers to perform a huge variety of tasks. Customers may also be interacting with the company's computers through the Internet, cash machines, touch screens in shopping malls and so on.

'Information' is a resource, but one that has completely different properties from other resources such as raw materials or stock. For one thing, it is not depleted when it is used. For another, it is difficult and usually undesirable to keep exclusive ownership of information. It is usually regarded as a shared resource within a company.

The challenge for management is to formulate an information management policy that will help them manage computing resources in an effective and profitable way, and maximise the benefits of information.

We'll look at four different strategic planning issues related to information systems:

- Consistency with business priorities;
- Centralisation vs. decentralisation;
- Different user needs;
- Hardware and software choices.

Consistency with business priorities

A company's information system strategy should be linked to its business plan. This may seem obvious, but in practice, it does not always happen. One method used to try and ensure that it does is to use an approach called the **critical success factors** (CSF) method. This encourages senior executives to identify the company's primary goals and what things must go right for the business to succeed. They then identify measures of performance for each of these CSFs and make sure that the information systems are in place to collect and use this information.

> ➤ **Discussion: Typical example of CSFs include improving customer service, improving supplier relationships, holding the right stock at the right time in the right quantity, and using human resources efficiently.**
>
> ➤ **What performance indicators could be used to measure better customer service?**
>
> ➤ **What are the critical success factors in your school, college or department? How are information systems used to collect information about performance indicators?**

Centralisation vs. decentralisation

Most organisations today retain a department for computing services known for example as the 'Information Systems Department'. This department will have the responsibility for the planning and control of processing, the maintenance of hardware and software and the development of new computerised information systems.

In some organisations, the various tasks connected with managing computer resources are all performed centrally by the Information Systems Department. In other organisations, many tasks are performed by individual departments in a so-called decentralised or 'distributed' system. A centralised system has the advantage of providing a centralised pool of expertise and better control over what hardware and software is purchased. A distributed system, however, allows users in individual departments to develop their own applications and lessens dependence on the central resource.

Different user needs

A typical medium- to large-sized organisation using computers will have a number of different types of users, each with their own different requirements, as shown in Figure 52.1.

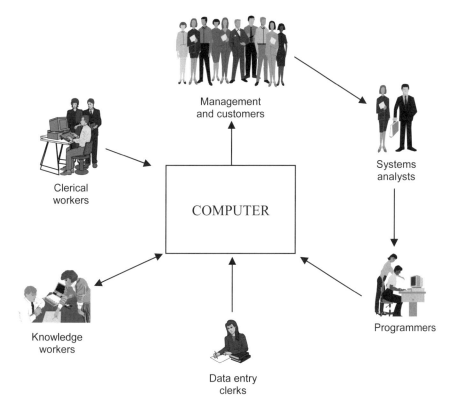

Figure 52.1: Different users in an organisation

Systems analysts, programmers and data entry clerks are computer users who interact with the computer system, but are distinct from 'end-users' who are the ultimate consumers of computer processing and information. Information systems fall into three major categories, each of which has different end-users:

- **Transaction processing systems**. Users: Clerical workers, salespeople, data entry clerks and customers.

- **Knowledge work systems**. Users: Middle managers, professional people such as accountants, engineers and graphic designers.

- **Management support systems**. Users: Senior managers.

End-users require software that is easy to use and which has enough features to help them to get their jobs done as efficiently as possible. They need hardware that is sufficiently powerful to run the software without frustrating delays.

> ➢ **A personnel manager in a large engineering company has asked one of her staff to produce a report showing which Universities they recruited from in the past five years, the proportion of those accepted out of the total interviewed, the proportion of men and women, and various other statistics. What software would be helpful in compiling this report?**

Hardware and software choices

With the trend towards distributed systems, there is a choice between allowing each department to purchase the hardware and software it considers most suitable for its own applications, or controlling all purchases from a central Information Systems Department. Generally the advantages of centralised control outweigh the disadvantages, and include the following:

- All hardware within the company will be compatible and can be linked in a company-wide network;
- Purchasing power is increased if high volumes are ordered by an organisation;
- The organisation is likely to get a better deal on maintenance contracts;
- Employees will not have to learn new systems if they move to another department;
- Training courses can be organised for people using the same software from many departments;
- Site licences can be purchased for software;
- There is better control over the use of unlicensed software;
- Data can be exchanged more easily between similar types of computer.

The term **platform** is used to describe the basic type of computer that an information system uses. A small business might for example choose between a platform based on an Intel chip (used on PCs) or a Motorola Power PC chip (used in Apple computers). The decision would depend on the characteristics of the application and the availability of software that runs on a particular platform. Upgrading to a more powerful computer in the same family costs money but in principle causes few technical difficulties, but moving between platforms is usually more complex because software written for one type of computer will generally not run on another.

The hardware would then be described as *incompatible*. *Compatible* hardware, on the other hand, means that the different hardware will all support the same data files and software. Likewise, software may be described as compatible if it can read data files written for different software. For example, new versions of software are sometimes incompatible with older versions, so that a file created in Word 2002, for example, cannot be read in Word 97. Similarly a file created on a Mac may not be readable on a PC.

Emulation software

One solution to the problem of incompatibility is to use **emulation software**. This software (if it is available) can be run on the user's existing hardware to make it function like a different computer. It then becomes possible for someone working, say, on an Apple Mac to read a file created on a PC and use PC software to manipulate it as required.

This has some advantages:

- You can read more file types, some of which may be specific to the other hardware platform
- You don't have to invest in new hardware in order to be able to read files sent from other sources

Emulation software also has disadvantages:

- It may run too slowly to be practical except for occasional emergency use
- The emulation software will occupy space on the disk and also take up memory when it is running
- You may lose the advantages of using specialised software designed for your hardware

Emulation software is not in common use today as many manufacturers are striving to achieve cross-platform compatibility.

Upgrading hardware and software

Many firms face a crucial challenge in the form of **legacy systems**: systems that have been passed down to the current users and IS staff. They are old, often technically obsolete systems that perform essential data processing such as accounting and customer billing. Many of these systems, written in COBOL in the 1960s and 70s, have been upgraded time and time again, using programming methods that are years out of date, and are technically fragile, difficult to maintain and impossible to understand. Because they still work, however, it may be difficult to get the funds to start from scratch with a new system.

Even companies with relatively new information systems face the constant problem of upgrades. Nothing stands still in computing – sometimes it seems as though no sooner have you bought a brand new PC to run your software than a new, better software version comes out that requires an even more powerful processor and twice as much memory to run it. When a company has upwards of a thousand PCs, the problem of upgrading becomes immense. Should everyone upgrade? Should no-one upgrade? Should selected departments upgrade?

Very likely some people would really benefit from the new features of upgraded software. On the other hand, documents created on the latest version of Word, for example, cannot be read in a previous version. This will inevitably cause problems.

> ➤ **Discussion: A school has the funds to equip a classroom with a new set of computers running the latest version of Windows. However, the other computers in the school are not powerful enough to run this version. What factors should the computer manager take into account when deciding what to do?**
>
> ➤ **What would you do if you were the computer manager?**

Future proofing

Is it possible to make such a shrewd choice of hardware and software that there will be no need to change it for years to come – to 'future proof' your purchases? Experience says a firm No. With processors still doubling in power every 18 months or so, and new versions of software appearing with monotonous regularity every year or two, most individuals and organisations resign themselves to the fact that regular upgrades will be necessary. The best strategy may be to buy hardware that has far more capability than is currently needed in anticipation of future need.

> ➤ **Discussion: What are the drawbacks of this strategy?**

Offers from TIME computer systems: Future proof?

Below are some offers from Time Computer Systems advertised over a seven-year period:

Date	Processor	RAM	Disk	Price
January 1996	75MHz Pentium	8Mb	850Mb	£1666
April 1997	166MHz Pentium	32Mb	2.1Gb	£1291
February 1998	233MHz Pentium	64Mb	6.4Gb	£1099
January 2000	500MHz Pentium	128Mb	20Gb	£1096
July 2002	AMD Athlon XP2000+	512Mb	80Gb	£699
February 2003	AMD Athlon XP2000+	512Mb	80Gb	£589

> ➤ **Discussion: Look up the latest offer from TIME Computer Systems. (Try the back of Thursday's OnLine section of the Guardian.)**

Exercises

1. 'If I need an I.T. system I buy whatever hardware and software I want without any regard to anyone.'
    This statement was made by a manager of a department in a company.
    Why is this an inappropriate approach in a large organisation? (6)
    NEAB IT05 Qu 7 Sample paper

2. A graphic designer makes use of a particular hardware platform and particular software packages. Her clients often send her files produced on computer systems that are incompatible with hers. One solution for the designer is to use emulation software.
    Describe **one** advantage and **one** limitation the designer will have if she pursues this solution. (4)
    AQA ICT5 Qu 2 June 2002

3. Hardware and software are often described as being "compatible" with other hardware or software.
    a. Describe the term *compatible* in this context. (2)
    b. An emulator can sometimes be used to achieve compatibility.
    Describe **one** advantage and **one** limitation of the use of emulation. (4)
    AQA ICT5 Qu 4 January 2003

Chapter 53 – Security and Backup Policies

Introduction

There are two main ways to ensure that ICT systems, once up and running, are protected from disaster, misuse or abuse. These are:

- Security measures;
- A personnel policy which covers data security and employee codes of conduct.

Under UK law, the responsibility for the security of the ICT assets of a company, including its hardware, networks, software, databases and so on lies not with the ICT department or the security officer, but with the company directors. They are *personally* responsible for the security of these assets. For this reason, they can be expected to give unequivocal support to the formulation and enforcement of an effective security policy.

Security policies were covered in Chapter 45. In this chapter we'll take a closer look at backup strategies.

Backup strategies

Some key issues need to be addressed when planning a backup strategy:

- **The frequency of the backup**. How often the data changes will affect how frequently it needs to be backed up.
- **The volume of data to be backed up**. Decisions need to be made as to whether all data will be backed up when the backup is made, or only data which has changed since the last backup. The volume of data will affect the time needed for the backup.
- **The storage medium to be used for backup**. A suitable medium such as cartridge tape needs to be chosen, depending on the volume of data to be backed up, the expense, and the convenience of the medium.
- **Where the backup will be stored**. The backup disk or tape needs to be stored in a secure location away from the main system. It is desirable to have a backup stored offsite in case of fire or theft.
- **The personnel given responsibility for backups**. Someone must be put in charge of seeing that the backup is done. When they are on holiday or away sick, someone else must be designated to take over responsibility.
- **Logging the backups**. A log of backups may be kept, and also a log of any problems that arise during the backup procedure. The problems then need to be addressed to ensure that the backup is properly done.
- **Testing of backup data**. It is essential to load the backup disk or tape every so often to make sure that the data can be recovered if the need arises.

Proper backup procedures are the first line of defence against disaster. Both software and data need to be backed up and stored safely, off-site or in a fire-proof safe. Data may need to be backed up at least once a day and taken off-site. Software only needs to be backed up when a change is made or a new version installed.

Many organisations, from hospitals and government departments to banks and manufacturers, are totally dependent on the data held in databases which are continually being updated. A comprehensive backup strategy is required.

Full backup

A full backup is a copy of all the files on a disk. This is a very safe strategy because it ensures that you have a copy of every program and every data file on the disk, and it is easy to restore if it ever becomes necessary. However a full backup takes a long time to complete and the computer cannot be used for anything else while it in progress.

Example: A large organisation holds all the data on its database on a 10Gb file server in the office. It uses the following backup strategy:

- The organisation has a service agreement with a local company under which engineers will be at the office in under two hours in the event of any problem.

- The file server contains two disk drives, 'mirrored disks' containing identical data. All transactions are written simultaneously to both disks, so that if one disk crashes, the other disk drive contains all the data. No further transactions are accepted until the disk drive is repaired or replaced by the Service Agency.

- Four backup tapes marked **Monday, Tuesday, Wednesday, Thursday** are stored in a fireproof safe in the office. Each night, the relevant day's tape is loaded, a backup program starts automatically at midnight and backs up the entire contents of the hard disk, which takes several hours. One person in the office (a young Business Studies graduate whose main job is Marketing) is in charge of checking the on-screen messages in the morning to ensure that the backup has completed successfully, and if not, the Service Agency is notified.

- Every Friday, the person responsible for the backup procedures takes the **Friday** tape home, and on Monday, brings back the tape from two Fridays ago to be overwritten the following Friday.

- The Service Agency is responsible for maintaining the hardware and replacing, say, a worn tape drive.

- Occasionally, the tape is tested by restoring it onto a spare machine provided by the agency to check that the data is in fact being correctly backed up and that the hard disk can be correctly restored to its previous state.

Incremental backup

With this type of backup, a full backup of the entire hard disk is made say once a week on Monday. On Tuesday, only those files which have been created or changed during the day are backed up. This backup tape or disk is carefully labelled 'Tuesday'. On Wednesday, only the files which have been changed or created on Wednesday are backed up, and so on.

This backup strategy is less time-consuming but more complex to restore, as all the backups have to be restored in the correct sequence.

Hardware for backups

For small quantities of data, removable disks are the simplest. Iomega's Zip drive sells for under £100 and takes 100Mb or 250Mb disks similar to floppy disks (less than £10 each). It can copy 100Mb of data in about 5 minutes.

Figure 53.1: Iomega Zip drive

For larger backups, tape is the preferred medium. A DAT tape drive with a capacity of 24Gb and more costs about £600 and tape cartridges cost from about £5 to £50 depending on capacity.

Figure 53.2: A DAT tape with a capacity of 24Gb

Case study: Back up that data

The simplest backup strategy is to copy the contents of your hard disk at the end of each day to a tape or removable disk. Keep Friday's backup for a month, and one backup each month for a year. To prevent mix-ups, give each tape or disk a serial number, and keep a log book. Once done, the backup tape or disk should be stored in a safe place.

You can reduce the volume and time by using 'compression' software, which comes with the tape or disk drive, and by only backing up data files. Software programs do not need to be backed up except when they are changed. If the backup is still unmanageable, you can reduce it by backing up only files which have changed since you last did a backup – an 'incremental' backup. A typical strategy would be to do a full backup on a Monday, and incrementals Tuesday to Friday.

"One small business did backups every day and stored them in a fireproof safe", says Colin Pearson, I.T. adviser at Business Link Staffordshire. "Then some thieves stole the computer and the safe, so they lost the lot."

Once the backup is made, your worries are not entirely over, as self-employed public relations consultant David Bridson discovered. He religiously backs up his data every night onto a removable optical disk. But some months ago he moved his e-mail database to a different directory on his hard disk, and forgot to tell the backup software. Recently, seeing that his hard disk was getting full, he deleted some redundant files.

"Of course, the directories I cleared out were the ones I'd moved all this valuable information to", he says. "I went to each of my five backups and found that none of them contained my up-to-date e-mail list."

Source: Paul Bray, Sunday Times 19 October 1997

On-line backup (RAID)

Thousands of organisations such as hospitals, banks, airlines, supermarkets etc. as well as smaller organisations cannot afford to lose even a few second's worth of data. How can they protect against disaster? The answer is that each transaction is written simultaneously to at least two and probably three different disks. Such a system is known as a drive array or RAID system (Redundant Array of Inexpensive Drives). The system is usually accompanied by software which gives the operator the option of switching over to the second disk automatically in the event of the first one failing. A third disk drive at some geographically remote location also records the data so that if one building is bombed the data is still safe.

Grandfather-father-son backups

Not all organisations use on-line databases. Many companies do their processing in 'batch mode', collecting transactions over a period of time and batching them into sets of say 50 documents. These can then be checked, control totals calculated and entered on a batch header record, and the data entered using a key-to-disk system. (Chapter 15.)

> ➤ **Discussion: What sort of organisation might use a batch processing system? Why?**

When batch processing is used, it is not necessary to back up all the data every night. The system uses 'generations' of master files, automatically creating a new 'generation' of master file each time the day's transactions are processed. To understand this process, imagine an equivalent manual system.

A class register for Lower VIa is written out in a register book in alphabetical order of students' names. Halfway through the term, it is decided to combine three classes into two, so a list of 5 extra students is given to the teacher of Lower VIa, who has to write out a brand new register. Unfortunately, three days later, the register disappears. Luckily, however, the teacher still has the old register and the list of names that were to be added, so the new register can be recreated.

In batch processing, transactions are typically processed once a day. A block diagram of the process is shown in Figure 53.3.

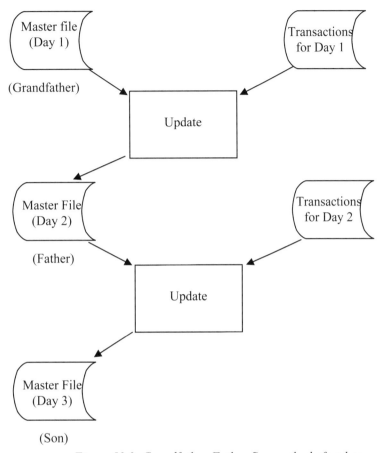

Figure 53.3: Grandfather-Father-Son method of update

When this method of processing is used, it is common to keep at least four generations of the master file along with the transactions that were used to update each generation. On the fifth day, the oldest generation of the master file (the 'grandfather') can be overwritten. Thus, there is always at least one generation of the master file and the corresponding transactions stored off-line in a secure fire-proof safe, with at least one pair off-site.

Exercises

1. A hospital information system holds program files which are rarely changed and large database files which are constantly changing.

    Describe a suitable backup strategy for this system, explaining what is backed up and when, together with the media and hardware involved. (8)

    NEAB IT05 Qu 8 1997

2. Describe **four** factors that need to be considered when a large company is devising a backup strategy for its information systems. (8)

    AQA ICT5 Qu 6 January 2003

Chapter 54 – Software Evaluation

Introduction

When a decision is made to computerise some aspect of the business, a feasibility study is carried out and then a detailed analysis is made of the user requirements. At some stage a decision has to be made whether to buy a software package 'off the shelf' or have software specially designed and developed either in-house or by outside consultants. In this chapter we'll be looking at methods of evaluating software packages to assess their suitability for the proposed task, and writing an evaluation report.

Choosing software

Suppose that you work for a small business that needs a computerised accounting system. You have been given the task of evaluating accounting packages and making a recommendation. Where do you start? Perhaps you may have heard the names of a few accounting packages, or can find out some names by browsing round PC World or asking a friend. The next thing you might try is to look up a supplier on the Internet – Sage, for example, has a well-known range of accounting packages.

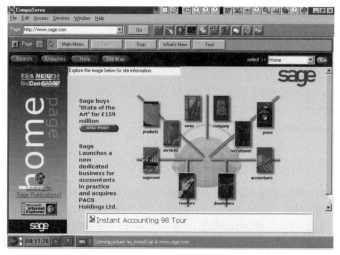

Figure 54.1: Getting information on accounting packages

Exploring a little further in the Sage site will bring up a guide which provides useful advice on finding a suitable package:

- DON'T walk into a shop or dealership and buy the cheapest thing on offer. Remember, it is not the PC that does the real work, it is the software and if you buy a system that is not suited to your business it could cost you a lot of time, money and effort later on. You should make this decision with great care because effectively, you will be running your business on the accounting system.

- DO start to collect some information on accounting software products and PCs and read some of the reviews published in computer magazines.

- DO talk to your accountant, who may be able to advise you about some packages. Information may also be available from professional bodies such as the Institute of Chartered Accountants.

- DO define what it is that you need an accounting software package to do. Do you want to run your whole system on it or just do some sales invoicing? Will you need to automate just the main ledgers or would you like to put sales order processing, purchase order processing and stock control onto the computer? Do you have any special procedures or requirements that you must stick to, whatever the system? Will you want to extract management information for use in decision-making?

When you have answered these questions, you can begin your search in earnest.

(Reproduced with permission from Sagesoft Ltd)

Tailoring the software

Sage emphasises that the first crucial step in selecting a suitable software package is to define exactly what the system must do to fulfil the requirements of the business. Cheaper packages bought off the shelf generally cannot be tailored to individual requirements. More expensive packages can often be configured to match user needs. It is no good buying a standard package that meets 80% of the user's needs but can't cope with the other, crucial, 20%.

Some software houses will be able to tailor an existing package to provide the extra functionality required. However, this is a dangerous option – Tony Collins in his book 'Crash' advises:

"With a standard package there is no such thing as a 'minor' code change. It is like trying to add an appendage to a human being. Imperfect as we are, we are tried and tested and are unlikely to work better with two hearts, or run faster with three legs. If you want to keep the project really simple, buy a package but *don't modify it.*"

Upgradability

A small business trying to keep a tight rein on overheads may be tempted to go for a good, simple and inexpensive package that serves their current needs. As the business expands, the package may no longer be adequate, and the pain of changing to a completely new system can be considerable. Therefore, it is desirable to choose a package that has a clear 'upgrade path' – many companies offer a range of upwardly-compatible packages so that data can easily be transferred to a more powerful package. The upgrades are offered at a special price to existing customers.

Other evaluation criteria

Several other factors need to be considered:

- **Compatibility with existing hardware and software**. Will the package run on existing hardware? Can files be easily transferred from existing systems without re-keying? Can files created in the package be exported to other systems in use in the company?
- **Resource requirements**. Will the system require expenditure on more powerful hardware, or extra staff to key in data?
- **Quality of documentation**. Are manuals supplied? Is there a good on-line help system?
- **Ease of learning**. Are tutorials supplied? Are books on the software available in bookshops? Are training courses available?
- **Ease of use**. Is it easy to use, for example using pull-down menus, icons, helpful error messages when you do something wrong?
- **Technical support**. Is support available? Is it very costly? Often, a technical support contract can add 50% or more to the price of a package, but without it no support at all will be given by the manufacturer.
- **Cost**. This includes the original cost of the package, technical support, and upgrades.
- **Performance**. The speed at which the package carries out critical operations can be measured using benchmark tests (see below). The new software must be more efficient than current methods.

Benchmark tests

A benchmark test, or performance test, can help determine the efficiency of the product. These tests involve comparing several different software packages by measuring the time that each one takes to perform various tasks. Computer magazines regularly publish the results of benchmark tests on different types of software.

Checking out the manufacturer

An important criterion in selecting a software package is the reputation of the manufacturer and the supplier: the relationship with the supplier can be crucial in getting the right package. It is important that the supplier understands how your business works and what the requirements are, and to provide support when problems arise. Consulting other users, reading magazine articles and visiting suppliers to discuss requirements are all ways of finding out who you can rely on.

Evaluation report

Once a thorough evaluation of possible software options has been made, an evaluation report may be written to document the performance of the software examined, and to make recommendations so that a decision can be made on what software to purchase.

The report will typically contain:

- An introduction stating the purpose of the report, and which software was evaluated;
- The methodology used to evaluate the software options;
- The actual evaluation, including the capabilities of the software, results of benchmark tests, upgrade facilities, compatibility with existing software base etc.
- Recommendations;
- Justifications for the recommended purchase.

Exercises

1. In groups of two or three students, carry out an evaluation of several similar packages e.g. word processing packages, spreadsheets, databases or graphics packages. Write an evaluation report and give a presentation of your recommendations for which package the school/college should invest in.

    New question

2. You are asked to evaluate a software package and produce an evaluation report.
    (a) Describe **four** criteria you would use to evaluate the package.   (8)
    (b) What is the function and content of an evaluation report?   (4)

    NEAB IT05 Qu 4 Sample paper

3. A company is about to change its accounting software. In order to evaluate the different packages available to them, they have drawn up a number of evaluation criteria.
    (a) Why are such evaluation criteria needed?   (2)
    (b) Explain the issues involved with each of the **three** evaluation criteria given below:
           Functionality
           User Support
           Hardware Resource Requirements.   (6)
    (c) Identify and describe **three** additional evaluation criteria that you might expect the company to include.   (6)

    NEAB IT05 Qu 8 1998

4. A system for the production of about one hundred thousand electricity bills per day is required. A number of alternative systems are available for purchase.

   The following features of each alternative system have been given numerical weightings to reflect their relative importance:

Feature	Weighting
A: purchase cost	5
B: maintenance and running costs	10
C: user friendliness of the software	3
D: bill printing speed	12
E: quality of printed output	8

   The required system is selected as follows:

Step 1	Rank each feature of each alternative system in order of merit.	For example, with regard to feature A, purchase cost, the most expensive system would be given a ranking of 1, the second most expensive a ranking of 2, and so on.
Step 2	Multiply each of these rankings by its respective weighting.	For example, with regard to feature E, which has a weighting of 8, the system with the worst printed output would have a computed value of (1 x 8), the system with the second worst printed output a computed value of (2 x 8) and so on.
Step 3	For each alternative system calculate a total of these computer values. The system with the largest total should be selected.	

   (a) Suggest a possible consequence of feature C being given a low weighting. (2)

   (b) Comment on the relative size of the weighting given to feature D in comparison to the other features. (2)

   (c) State **three** advantages of this method of selecting a computer system. (3)

   (d) Identify **four** factors other than those listed which should be taken into account before a system is purchased. Justify your suggestions. (8)

   London Computing Paper 2 Qu 12 1997

5. Give **four** reasons for producing an evaluation report when considering alternative software solutions to a particular problem. (4)

   AQA ICT5 Qu 2 January 2003

Chapter 55 – Data Modelling

Traditional file approach

Most organisations began information processing on a small scale, buying a computer for perhaps one or two individual applications, and then computerising other departments one by one. Applications were developed independently, and files of information relevant to one particular department were created and processed by dozens or even hundreds of separate programs. This situation led to several problems:

- **Data redundancy.** The same data was duplicated in many different files. For example, details of a salesman's name, address and pay rate might be held on a payroll file for calculating the payroll. The same data may be held on a file in the Personnel department along with a lot of other personal data, and in the Sales Department which has a program to keep track of each salesman's record and performance.

- **Data inconsistency.** When the same items of data are held in several different files, the data has to be updated in each separate file when it changes. The Payroll Department, for example, may change the commission rates paid to salesmen but the Sales Department file may fail to update its files and so be producing reports calculated with out-of-date figures.

- **Lack of data integrity.** 'Data integrity' refers to the correctness or reliability of data. Validation is one way of improving data integrity. For example, a range check may be applied to monthly salaries being entered so that it is not possible to enter, for example £12,500 instead of £1,250. Of course, it is still possible to make data entry errors and the more times the data is entered on different files, the greater are the chances that an error will be made somewhere.

- **Program-data dependence.** Every computer program in each department has to specify exactly what data fields constitute a record in the file being processed. Any change to the format of the data fields – for example, adding a new field or changing the length of a field – means that every program which uses that file has to be changed, since the file format is specified within each program.

- **Lack of flexibility.** In such a system, when information of a non-routine nature is needed, it can take weeks to assemble the data from the various files and write new programs to produce the required reports.

- **Data was not shareable.** If one department had data that was required by another department, it was awkward to obtain it. A second copy of the file could be made, but this would obviously soon lead to problems of inconsistency. If the same file was used, it would almost certainly be necessary to add extra fields for the new application, and that would mean the original programs would have to be changed to reflect the new file structure.

The database approach

In an attempt to solve these problems, the concept of a database was born.

A **database** is defined as a collection of non-redundant data shareable between different applications.

All the data belonging to the entire organisation would be centralised in a common pool of data, accessible by all applications. This solved the problems of redundancy and inconsistency, but two major problems remained to be addressed.

- **Unproductive maintenance.** Programs were still dependent on the structure of the data, so that when one department needed to add a new field to a particular file, all other programs accessing that file had to be changed.

- **Lack of security**. All the data in the database, even confidential or commercially sensitive data, was accessible by all applications.

The Database Management System (DBMS)

A DBMS is a layer of software inserted between the applications and the data, which attempts to solve these problems. Two essential features of the DBMS are:

- Program-data independence, whereby the storage structure of the data is hidden from each application/user;

- Restricted user access to the data – each user is given a limited view of the data according to need.

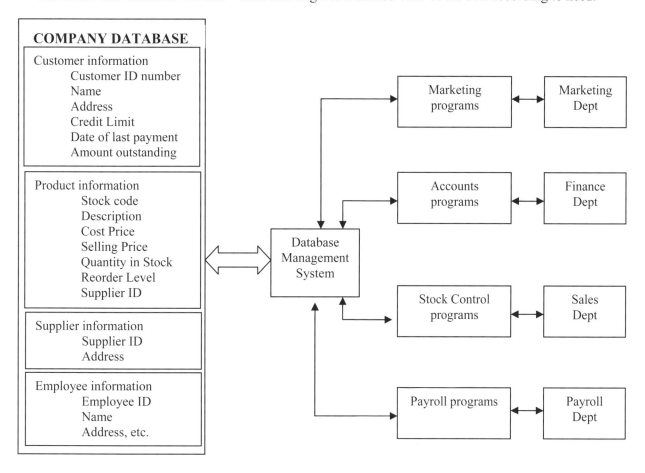

Figure 55.1: The DBMS acts as an interface between application programs and data

The conceptual data model

The first stage in designing a database is to identify and state what data needs to be held. Figure 55.1 shows some of the data items that may be required for some of the applications required by an organisation such as a Department store.

From the statement of data requirements a **conceptual data model** is produced. This describes how the data elements in the database are to be grouped. Three terms are used in building a picture of the data requirements.

1. An **entity** is a thing of interest to an organisation about which data is to be held. Examples of entities include Customer, Employee, Stock Item, Supplier.

2. An **attribute** is a property or characteristic of an entity. Examples of attributes associated with a Customer include Customer ID, Surname, Initials, Title, Address, Credit Limit.

3. A **relationship** is a link or association between entities. An example is the link between Dentist and Patient; one dentist has many patients, but each patient only has one dentist.

This conceptual data model is created without specifying what type of database system will eventually be used to implement the system.

Types of relationship

There are only three different 'degrees' of relationship between two attributes. A relationship may be

- **One-to-one**   Examples of such a relationship include the relationship between Husband and Wife, or between Householder and Main Residence.

- **One-to-many**   Examples include the relationship between Mother and Children, between Customer and Order, between Borrower and Library Book.

- **Many-to-many**   Examples include the relationship between Student and Course, between Stock Item and Supplier, between Film and Film Star.

Entity-relationship diagrams

An entity-relationship diagram is a diagrammatic way of representing the relationships between the entities in a database. To show the relationship between two entities, both the **degree** and the **name** of the relationship need to be specified. E.g. In the first relationship shown below, the **degree** is one-to-one, the **name** of the relationship is *Drives*:

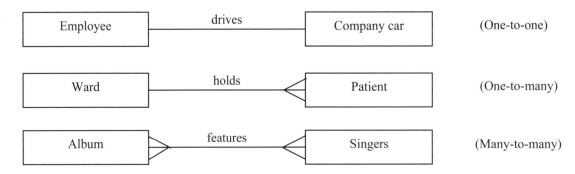

Figure 55.2: Entity relationships

Sometimes it can be tricky to establish the degree of the relationship. For example, several employees may use the same company car at different times. A single employee may change the company car that he uses. The relationship will depend upon whether the data held refers to the current situation, or whether it is a historical record. The assumption has been made above that the database is to record the current car driven by an employee.

Example:

The data requirements for a hospital in-patient system are defined as follows:

A hospital is organised into a number of wards. Each ward has a ward number and a name recorded, along with a number of beds in that ward. Each ward is staffed by nurses. Nurses have their staff number and name recorded, and are assigned to a single ward.

Each patient in the hospital has a patient identification number, and their name, address and date of birth are recorded. Each patient is under the care of a single consultant and is assigned to a single ward. Each consultant is responsible for a number of patients. Consultants have their staff number, name and specialism recorded.

State four entities for the hospital in-patient system and suggest an identifier for each of these entities.

Draw an entity-relationship diagram to show the relationship between the entities.

Answer:

Entity	**Identifier**
WARD	Ward number
NURSE	Staff number
PATIENT	Patient identification number
CONSULTANT	Staff number

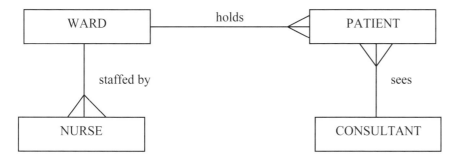

Exercises

1. A library plans to set up a database to keep track of its members, stock and loans.
   (a) State an identifier for each of the entities MEMBER, STOCK and LOAN. (3)
   (b) Draw an entity-relationship diagram showing the relationships between the entities. (3)
   (New question)

2. What is meant by program-data independence in the context of a database management system? (2)
   AEB Computing Paper 2 Qu 2 1994

3. A vet has a database to keep track of the animals seen at the surgery.
   (a) Name two entities in this database, and suggest an identifier for each one. (2)
   (b) Name FOUR attributes for each of the entities. (4)
   (c) What is the relationship between the two entities? (You may use a diagram). (2)
   (New question)

4. Explain, with an example of each, what is meant by:
   (a) data consistency;
   (b) data integrity;
   (c) data redundancy. (6)
   (New question)

Chapter 56 – Relational Database Design

What is a relational database?

There are several different types of Database Management System available. The most common type of DBMS is the **relational database**, widely used on all systems from micros to mainframes. In a relational database, data is held in tables (also called relations) and the tables are linked by means of common fields.

Conceptually then, one row of a table holds one record. Each column in the table holds one field or attribute.

e.g. A table holding data about an entity BOOK may have the following rows and columns:

BOOK

Accession Number	DeweyCode	Title	Author	DatePublished
88	121.9	Let's Cook!	Chan, C	1992
123	345.440	Electricity	Glendenning, V	1995
300	345.440	Riders	Cooper,J	1995
657	200.00	Greek in 3 weeks	Stavros,G	1990
777	001.602	I.T. in Society	Laudon, K	1994
etc				

Figure 56.1: A table in a relational database

There is a standard notation for describing a table in a relational database. For example, to describe the table shown above, you would write

> BOOK (AccessionNumber, DeweyCode, Title, Author, DatePublished)

Note that:

> The entity name is shown in uppercase letters;
>
> The key field (unique identifier) is underlined;
>
> The attributes are shown in brackets, separated by commas.

Linking database tables

Tables may be linked through the use of a common field. This field must be a key field of one of the tables, and is known as a **foreign key** in the second table. An example best illustrates this.

In a library database, two entities named BOOK and BORROWER have been identified. An entity-relationship diagram may be used to describe the relationship between these two entities.

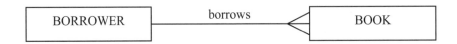

Figure 56.2: One-to-many relationship between BORROWER and BOOK

The BORROWER table can be described using standard notation as follows:

BORROWER (BorrowerID, name, address)

In order to link the two entities, the key field Borrower ID needs to be added to the BOOK table as a *foreign key*. The BOOK table can be described as

BOOK (AccessionNumber, DeweyCode, Title, Author, DatePublished, *BorrowerID, DateDue*)

Note that a foreign key is shown in italics.

In practice, since only a very small proportion of books are on loan at any one time, it would be sensible to have a third table holding data about books on loan, who had borrowed them and when they were due back. The three tables would then look like this:

BORROWER (BorrowerID, name, address)

BOOK (AccessionNumber, DeweyCode, Title, Author, DatePublished)

LOAN (AccessionNumber, *BorrowerID*, DateDue)

The entity-relationship diagram would then look like this:

Figure 56.3: Entity-relationship diagram for a library database

> ➤ **Discussion: The model above assumes that the LOAN record will be deleted when a book is returned. If this is not going to be done, what adjustments will have to be made to the entity-relationship diagram and LOAN table?**

Normalisation

Normalisation is a process used to come up with the best possible design for a relational database. Tables should be organised in such a way that:

- No data is unnecessarily duplicated (i.e. the same data held on more than one table).

- Data is consistent throughout the database (e.g. Mr Bradley's address is not recorded as The White House, Sproughton on one table and as 32 Star Lane in another. Consistency should be an automatic consequence of not holding any duplicated data.)

- The structure of each table is flexible enough to allow you to enter as many or as few items (for example, books borrowed by a particular person) as you want to.

- The structure should enable a user to make all kinds of complex queries relating data from different tables.

We will look at three stages of normalisation known as first, second and third normal form.

First normal form

Definition: A table is in first normal form if it contains no repeating attributes or groups of attributes.

Let's look at a simple example of two entities STUDENT and COURSE. A student can take several courses, and each course has several students attending. The relationship can be represented by the entity-relationship diagram.

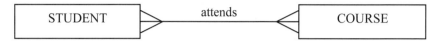

Figure 56.4: The many-to-many relationship between entities STUDENT and COURSE

Sample data to be held in the database is shown in the table below:

STUDENT

student number	student name	date of birth	sex	course number	course name	lecturer number	lecturer name
12345	Heathcote,R	20-08-77	M	EC6654	A-Level Computing	T345267	Glover,T
22433	Head,J	13-02-77	F	EC6654	A-Level Computing	T345267	Glover,T
				HM7756	A-Level Music	T773351	Reader,B
				AD1121	Pottery	T876541	
66688	Hargrave,R	13-09-54	M	BM3390	HNC Business	T666758	Newman,P
				HM7756	A-Level Music	T773351	Reader,B

The two tables STUDENT and COURSE will be represented in standard notation as

     STUDENT (<u>student number</u>, student name, date of birth, sex)

     COURSE (<u>course number</u>, course name, lecturer number, lecturer name)

The question now is, how can the relationship between these two tables be shown? How can we hold the information about which students are doing which courses?

The two tables need to be linked by means of a common field, but the problem is that because this is a many-to-many relationship, whichever table we put the link field into, there needs to be *more than one* field.

e.g.   STUDENT (<u>student number</u>, student name, date of birth, sex, *course number*)

is no good because the student is doing several courses, so which one would be mentioned?

Similarly,   COURSE (<u>course number</u>, course name, lecturer number, lecturer name, *student number*)

is no good either because each course has a number of students taking it.

One obvious solution (and unfortunately a bad one) springs to mind. How about allowing space for 3 courses on each student record?

     STUDENT (<u>student number</u>, student name, date of birth, sex, *course1, course2, course3*)

> **Discussion: Why is this not a good idea?**

What we have engineered is a repeating attribute – anathema in 1st normal form. In other words, the field course number is repeated 3 times. The table is therefore NOT in first normal form.

It would be represented in standard notation with a line over the repeating attribute:

     STUDENT (<u>student number</u>, student name, date of birth, sex, course number)

To put the data into first normal form, the repeating attribute must be removed. In its place, the field course number becomes part of the primary key in the student table. The tables are now as follows:

     STUDENT (<u>student number</u>, student name, date of birth, sex, <u>course number</u>)

     COURSE (<u>course number</u>, course name, lecturer number, lecturer name)

> ➤ **Discussion: What is a primary key? Why does course number have to be part of the primary key?**

The two tables STUDENT and COURSE now in first normal form, look like this:

STUDENT

student number	student name	date of birth	sex	course number
12345	Heathcote,R	20-08-77	M	EC6654
22433	Head,J	13-02-77	F	EC6654
22433	Head,J	13-02-77	F	HM7756
22433	Head,J	13-02-77	F	AD1121
66688	Hargrave,R	13-09-54	M	BM3390
66688	Hargrave,R	13-09-54	M	HM7756

COURSE

course number	course name	lecturer number	lecturer name
EC6654	A-Level Computing	T345267	Glover,T
HM7756	A-Level Music	T773351	Reader,B
AD1121	Pottery	T876541	
BM3390	HNC Business	T666758	Newman,P

> ➤ **Discussion: Why is this a better way of holding the data than having one table with the following structure?**
>
> **STUDENT (student number, student name, date of birth, sex, *course1, course2, course3*)**
>
> **If student Head, J decides to take up A Level Art, what changes need to be made to the data?**
>
> **How will we find the names of all students doing A-Level Computing?**
>
> **What are the weaknesses of this table structure?**

Second normal form – Partial key dependence test

Definition: A table is in second normal form (2NF) if it is in first normal form and no column that is not part of a primary key is dependent on only a portion of the primary key.

This is sometimes expressed by saying that a table in second normal form contains no partial dependencies.

The tables above are not in second normal form. For example, Student name is dependent only on Student number and not on Course number. To put the tables into second normal form, we need to introduce a third table (relation) that acts as a link between the entities Student and Course.

The tables are now as follows:

STUDENT (student number, student name, date of birth, sex)

STUDENT_TAKES(student number, course number)

COURSE (course number, course name, lecturer number, lecturer name)

Dealing with a Many-to-Many relationship

As you get more practice in database design, you will notice that *whenever* two entities have a many-to-many relationship, you will *always* need a link table 'in the middle'. Thus

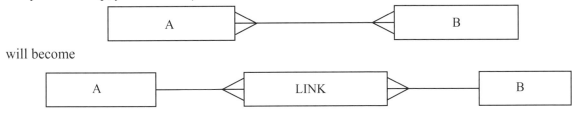

will become

Figure 56.5: A 'link' table is needed in a many-to-many relationship

Third normal form – Non-key dependence test

Definition: A table in third normal form contains no 'non-key dependencies'.

Looking at the COURSE table, the lecturer name is dependent on the lecturer number, not on the course number. It therefore needs to be removed from this relation and a new relation created:

LECTURER (<u>lecturer number</u>, lecturer name)

The database, now in third normal form, consists of the following tables:

STUDENT (<u>student number</u>, student name, date of birth, sex)

STUDENT_TAKES (<u>student number</u>, <u>course number</u>)

COURSE (<u>course number</u>, course name, lecturer number)

LECTURER (<u>lecturer number</u>, lecturer name)

This is the optimum way of holding the data, with no attributes being duplicated anywhere. In any database work that you do, you should always make sure you have designed the tables in such a way that they are in THIRD NORMAL FORM.

Comparing a flat-file system with a relational database

From the example above you will have seen that a relational database is able to create **links** between tables representing different entities such as STUDENT and COURSE, through the use of **foreign keys**. *A flat-file system is not able to create links between tables* and is therefore only useful for very simple databases which contain information about just one entity. It is impossible to 'normalise' a database in a flat-file system, since this involves correctly establishing links between tables.

Flat-file systems do not have any of the sophisticated features of a full DBMS such as the ability to set individual user access rights, or allow several people to access the database at the same time.

Exercises

1. Data on patient prescriptions are held by a GP's surgery in the following form:

PRESCRIPTION

Patient ID	Patient Name	Date of Birth	Address	Date of prescription	Drug ID	Drug Name	Dosage	Manufacturer
111	Naylor E	12-9-76	76 Church St, Hull	2-9-96 5-12-96 3-4-97	AS12 AS12 BS03	Aspirin Aspirin Migril	2 tablets 3 tablets 2 tablets	Bayer Bayer Wellcome
123	Jones R	23-9-55	23 Bay Ave Hull	5-12-96	AR14	Arnica	2 tablets	Boots
234	Leech M	4-8-77	Reckitt Hall Cottingham	3-5-97	AS12	Aspirin	2 tablets	Bayer

(a) Draw an entity-relationship diagram showing the relationships between the entities PATIENT, DRUG and PRESCRIPTION. (3)

(b) Describe the three relations needed to hold the data in a relational database in second normal form. (7)

New question

308

2. The manager of a video hire shop uses a relational database management system to operate the business. Separate database files hold details of customers, video films and loans. Customers can hire as many films as they wish.

    (a) For each of the files mentioned above identify the key fields and list other appropriate fields that would be required to enable this system to be maintained with minimum redundancy. (6)

    (b) Describe **three** advantages of using a relational database rather than a flat-file information storage system. (6)

    NEAB IT02 Qu 7 1996

3. The data requirements for a booking system are defined as follows.

    An agency arranges booking of live bands for a number of clubs. Each band is registered with the agency and has its name (unique) recorded, together with the number of musicians, the type of music played and hiring fee. Each band is managed by a manager. A manager may manage several bands. Each manager is assigned an identification number and managers have their name, address and telephone number recorded. Each club is assigned an identification number and clubs have their name, address and telephone number recorded.

    The agency records details of each booking made between a band and a club for a given date. A band will never have more than one booking on any particular date.

    (a) In database modelling, what is:

        (i) an attribute; (1)

        (ii) a relationship? (1)

    (b) Four entities for the booking system are Manager, Club, Band and Booking.

        (i) Suggest an identifier, with justification, for **each** of the entities Manager, Club and Band. (3)

        (ii) Describe **four** relationships involving the entities Manager, Club, Band and Booking that can be inferred from the given data requirements. (4)

    (c) A relational database is to be used. Describe tables for the following entities underlining the primary key in each case:

        (i) Manager; (2)

        (ii) Band; (4)

        (iii) Booking. (5)

    AEB Computing Paper 2 Qu 12 1996

4. A company sports centre uses a database management system to operate a membership and fixture system. Normally members register for at least three sports, although they can play any of the sports offered by the centre. Fixtures against many other organisations are arranged in a wide range of sports involving a large number of teams.

    (a) Name **three** database files you would expect to find in this system. (3)

    (b) For each of the database files you have named, list the fields required to enable this system to be maintained with minimum redundancy. (6)

    (c) Draw a diagram to show the relationship between the database files named in part (a). (3)

    (d) Describe **three** reports that the system might be required to produce. (3)

    (e) The manager of the centre intends to send out personalised letters to each of the members. This is to be done using the mail-merge facility offered by a word-processor in conjunction with the database. Explain how this is achieved. (4)

    NEAB IT02 Specimen Paper Qu 10

Chapter 57 – Database Management

Introduction

The pooling of information, software, and computer power is very useful but it does involve potential problems. There is the danger that one user will damage or change data used by other people without their knowledge; there is the question of how to protect confidential information; there may be problems if more than one person tries to change the same item of data at the same time. If a hardware failure occurs, everyone using the database is affected, and recovery procedures must ensure that no data is lost.

In order to minimise the potential hazards, a group known as **database administration** (or a person in charge of the group, known as the **database administrator**) is responsible for supervising both the database and the use of the DBMS.

Database Administration (DBA)

The DBA's tasks will include the following:

1. The design of the database. After the initial design, the DBA must monitor the performance of the database, and if problems surface (such as a particular report taking an unacceptably long time to produce), appropriate changes must be made to the database structure.

2. Keeping users informed of changes in the database structure that will affect them; for example, if the size or format of a particular field is altered or additional fields added.

3. Maintenance of the **data dictionary** (see below) for the database, and responsibility for establishing conventions for naming tables, columns, indexes and so on.

4. Implementing access privileges for all users of the database; that is, specifying which items can be accessed and/or changed by each user.

5. Allocating passwords to each user.

The data dictionary

The data dictionary is a 'database about the database'. It will contain information such as:

• What tables and columns are included in the present structure;

• The names of the current tables and columns;

• The characteristics of each item of data, such as its length and data type;

• Any restrictions on the value of certain columns;

• The meaning of any data fields that are not self-evident; for example, a field such as 'course type';

• The relationships between items of data;

• Which programs access which items of data, and whether they merely read the data or change it.

The Database Management System (DBMS)

The DBMS is an application program that provides an interface between the operating system and the user in order to make access to the data as simple as possible. It has several other functions as well, and these are described below.

1. **Data storage, retrieval and update.** The DBMS must allow users to store, retrieve and update information as easily as possible, without having to be aware of the internal structure of the database.
2. **Creation and maintenance of the data dictionary**.
3. **Managing the facilities for sharing the database.** The DBMS has to ensure that problems do not arise when two people simultaneously access a record and try to update it.
4. **Backup and recovery.** The DBMS must provide the ability to recover the database in the event of system failure.
5. **Security.** The DBMS must handle password allocation and checking, and the 'view' of the database that a given user is allowed.

Querying the database

Different database systems all have their own way of performing **queries** to extract data from the database. However all perform similar functions, allowing the user to:

- Combine into one table the information from two or more related tables;
- Select the fields that are to be shown in the 'Answer' table;
- Specify criteria for searching on; e.g. find the names and addresses of all club members whose subscriptions are due;
- Save the query so that it can be executed whenever necessary;
- Save the 'Answer' table so that it can be displayed or used as the basis for a report or a mail shot, for example.

The figure below shows a **query by example** window in the Access database.

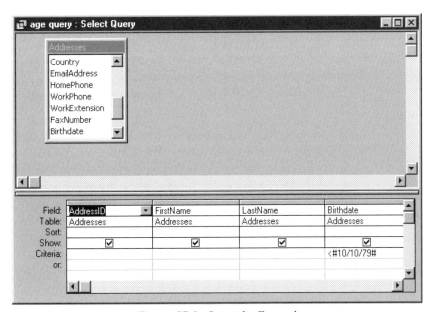

Figure 57.1: Query by Example

Using SQL

When a user constructs a query using a **query by example** form like the one shown above, the resultant query is automatically coded by Access into statements in **SQL**, or **Structured Query Language**. This is a data manipulation language that has been supported by many mainframe and minicomputers and more recently by PCs as well. The SQL for the query performed above, for example, can be viewed using a menu option in Access and is as shown below:

```
SELECT Addresses.AddressID, Addresses.FirstName, Addresses.LastName,
Addresses.Birthdate
FROM Addresses
WHERE (((Addresses.Birthdate)<#10/10/79#));
```

Client-server database

Many modern databases management systems provide an option for **client-server** operation. Using a client/server DBMS on a network, **DBMS server software** runs on the network server. This server software processes requests for data searches, sorts and reports that originate from the **DBMS client software** running on individual workstations. For example, a car dealer might want to search the manufacturer's database to find out whether there are any cars of a particular specification available. The DBMS client refers this request to the DBMS server, which searches for the information and sends it back to the client workstation. Once the information is at the workstation, the dealer can sort the list and produce his own customised report. If the DBMS did not have client-server capability, the entire database would be copied to the workstation and software held on the workstation would search for the requested data – involving a large amount of time being spent on transmitting irrelevant data and probably a longer search using a less powerful machine.

The advantages of a client-server database are, therefore:

- an expensive resource (powerful computer and large database) can be made available to a large number of users;

- client stations can, if authorised, update the database rather than just view the data;

- the consistency of the database is maintained because only one copy of the data is held (on the server) rather than a copy at each workstation;

- the database processing is normally carried out by the server, with the query being sent by a client station to the server and the results assembled by the server and returned to the client station;

- communication time between client and server is minimised because only the results of a query, not the entire database, is transmitted between the server and client;

- relevant programs and report formats can be held on client workstations and customised for a particular department.

Sage Accounting software, for example, has a client-server version. The Server Network Installation procedure installs the software and data files on the server. The Client version of the software is then installed at each workstation. Report formats for Stock, Invoices, Customers etc can be stored locally on the relevant client workstations where they can be customised and altered. Each client workstation is allocated access rights to particular files on the database; it may be possible for example to view stock levels, but not alter them from one workstation, ('read only access') to make stock adjustments from another workstation, ('read-write access'), or have no access at all to Customer account records from, say, a workstation in the warehouse.

Exercises

1. A college library uses a relational database management system to operate a membership and loans system. Staff and students can borrow as many books as they wish at any given time.

   (a) Name **three** database tables that you would expect to find in this system. In each case, identify the columns and keys required to enable this system to be maintained with minimum redundancy. (6)

   (b) Draw an entity-relationship diagram to show the links between the database tables named in part (a). (3)

   (c) Describe the capabilities of the relational database management system that might be used to identify and output details of overdue loans. (6)

   NEAB IT02 Qu 7 1997

2. (a) Briefly explain the principal differences between a relational database and a flat-file system. (4)

   (b) What is meant by data consistency, data redundancy and data independence? (3)

   (c) Describe **two** distinct security procedures you would expect to find in relational database management systems. (2)

   (d) Describe briefly **three** responsibilities of a database administrator. (6)

   New question

3. As an ICT manager in a medium sized company, you have been asked to create a job specification for a database administrator.

   (a) Describe **three** responsibilities you would include in this specification. (6)

   (b) The database that this person will be in charge of is a client/server database.

   Describe **two** advantages of using this type of database over a non-client/server database. (4)

   AQA ICT5 Qu 7 June 2002

Chapter 58 – Communication and Information Systems

Centralised processing systems

Until the 1970s, most organisations using computers were using **centralised** computer systems, with a mainframe computer doing all the processing for the whole company. Sometimes, on-line access to the mainframe computer would be possible from distant 'dumb' terminals – so-called because the terminals consisted of just a screen and a keyboard and no processor of their own. A similar type of centralised processing is still in use for some applications: banks, for example, use ATMs (Automated Teller Machines), a form of terminal containing a microprocessor which dispenses cash and enables customers to query their accounts. The ATMs are connected to a remote central computer which can be accessed from any ATM in the country.

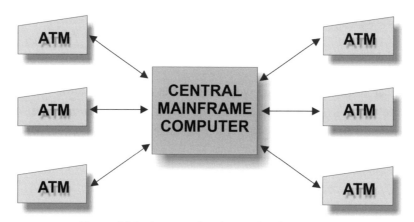

Figure 58.1: An example of centralised processing

Dispersed systems

As the price of hardware dropped, it became more cost-effective to move the processing power to where it was needed, often on individual users' desks. At first, as applications such as spreadsheets and word processors led to an explosion in the popularity of microcomputers, large numbers of standalone computers were to be found throughout an organisation, each running software suitable for a particular application or department but without the ability to communicate with one another. This arrangement could be termed a 'dispersed system'. The shortcomings of this arrangement soon became apparent, however.

> ➤ **Discussion: What were the advantages of having a number of standalone computers instead of having all the processing done on a central mainframe computer with remote terminals connected to it?**
> ➤ **What are the drawbacks of this arrangement?**
> ➤ **How can these drawbacks be overcome?**

Today, these microcomputers are commonly linked by means of cables and telecommunications into one or more types of **network**, allowing what is known as a 'distributed' system. There is a great variety of different types of network, and they can be categorised broadly into local, wide area and public networks.

Local area networks (LANs)

A local area network consists of a number of computers in the same building or site, connected by cables. No telecommunications lines are needed. Such an arrangement has many advantages over standalone computers:

- It permits the shared use of facilities such as printers, scanners and hard disk space.

- Communication between users becomes possible and, using software such as Lotus Notes, many workers can work on the same document at the same time.

- Software can be loaded on the file server and used by everyone on the network. When it is upgraded, new software has to be loaded only once instead of onto every machine.

- All users can have access to a database.

- Backup of all data held on a central file server can be done automatically every night.

Frequently, one of the facilities of a LAN is a **gateway** – hardware and software which gives all network users access to other networks.

> ➤ **Discussion: Is data MORE or LESS secure on a network than on standalone computers? Why?**

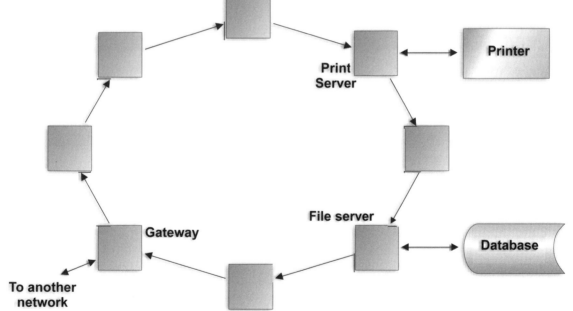

Figure 58.2: A local area network

Client-server and peer-to-peer networks

Most networks, except very small ones, operate on a client-server system. The 'clients' are normally microcomputers with their own processing power, connected to the file server which holds software and data. When a client wants to use a word processing package or a CAD package, for example, the software is downloaded into the client's RAM. Printing tasks may be handled by a print server, which queues the output from all the machines in the network and passes it to the printer. Both processing power and data may be distributed between the various machines on the network. Backup and security will be handled by the server.

Small networks of no more than 10 computers may use a peer-to-peer configuration, with none of the computers being in control of the network. Software may be held on any of the computers and made available to any other machine on the network. This does have the effect of slowing down the speed at which the software runs, but enables computer users in a small office to share disk space, software and data.

The relative benefits of client-server and peer-to-peer networks are summarised in Table 29.4 in Chapter 29.

Wide area networks (WANs)

Large organisations rely on wide area networks for communication and data exchange, not only between branches within the organisation but also between organisations. Booking an airline ticket or paying for goods by credit card are just two examples of transactions that would be impossible without wide area networks.

Distributed processing

With the growth of powerful telecommunications networks, organisations moved away from having a central mainframe to installing minicomputers and microcomputers at remote sites. These distributed processors directly serve local and regional branches and are generally linked together in networks. The dispersion of computers among multiple sites so that local computers can handle local processing needs is called **distributed processing**.

Case study: Pubs get a new round of touch tills

Many pub and restaurant customers can soon expect a slicker service as a new wave of computerised tills reach Britain's busiest bars and cafes.

Touch screen terminals promise to end those minor irritations which can spoil a night out, such as waiting ages for a drink or getting the wrong side order with a meal. Greenalls, a leading leisure company, has begun installing 1,000 InnTouch terminals in its bars and restaurants, which include the Henry's chain, Millers Kitchens and Bygone Inns.

The new tills allow bar staff to simply touch a symbol for each drink ordered and quickly provide the total cost. When a customer orders food, staff will touch a symbol for the main course and then move on to a second screen with all the possible side orders. If a customer orders steak, for example, the screen will show symbols for salads, onion rings, mushrooms and all other accompaniments.

"We expect the tills to speed up customer service by 40 per cent," says Tim Kowalski, Greenalls' financial director. With the new tills and back-up services costing £3 million, Greenalls will be looking for more than improved customer relations from its investment. The tills are linked to a computer in the manager's office at each property and that PC is linked by modem to the 32-bit Windows-based Innmaster system at Head Office.

The system will enable the company to gather immediate information about food and drinks sales, and this will inform decisions on changing menus or launching promotions. "While analysing food sales, for example, we noticed that Wall Street, a busy young persons' pub in Preston, was selling an average of only ten rounds of garlic bread per week," reports Kowalski. "This was at odds with sales in similar houses. We phoned the manager who hadn't realised this shortfall and he was able to brief waiters and waitresses. Consequently, sales increased by 40 to 50 rounds a week which, at a retail price of £1.20 per portion, could add £2,500 to annual sales."

The system also enables managers to monitor staff performance. Gail Pritchard, manager of Off the Wall, Chester, says: "We ran a promotion on Miller Draught with a £10 incentive to the staff member turning in the best performance each shift, and I was able to get an instant printout of everyone's performance.

Touch screens are logical and incredibly fast. They are a huge asset for us, and the staff like them."

Source: Tony Dawe, The Times 18 February 1998

> ➢ **Discussion: Is this a distributed or a centralised system? Where is the processing performed at each stage?**
> ➢ **Describe some of the advantages of the new system.**

Distributed systems may be organised in many different ways. Decisions have to be made on where to locate both the processing power and the databases, and how to connect the nodes (host computers and workstations) of the network. Distributed systems may extend over several levels, with some processing taking place at many different levels. In the case study above, processing is taking place at only two levels: local managers' offices and Head Office. In a large organisation such as for example Ford Motor Company which has offices and sites all over the world, there may be six or more levels over which processing is distributed, as shown in Figure 58.3.

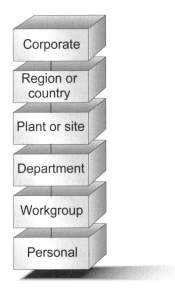

Figure 58.3: Possible distribution of systems in an organisation

Distributed databases

Although early distributed systems generally worked with a single centralised database, over time the smaller local systems began to store local databases as well. However, local branches frequently still need access to the main company database, which may be held in a different country altogether. Maintaining on-line access to a central database from all over the world can be very expensive – and so the next logical step was to distribute the central database to local processors. A mechanism is then needed to ensure the several versions of the database are properly updated, that the integrity of data is maintained (i.e. that different versions of the data are not held in different places) and that security is maintained.

A **distributed database** is one that is stored in more than one physical location. There are three main ways of distributing a database.

1. The central database can be partitioned so that each remote processor has the data on its own customers, stock, etc.

2. The entire database is duplicated at each remote site.

In both these cases, the two databases have to be reconciled with each other. This is usually done by updating the central database each night to reflect local changes made the previous day.

3. The central database contains only an index to entries which are held on local databases. This system is used for very large databases like the FBI's National Crime Information Centre. A query to the central database identifies the location where the full record is held. The National Westminster Bank uses a similar system to hold details on all its customers.

A variation of this system is not to hold an index, and to simply poll all remote databases until the required record is found. The complete record is then transferred to the local computer that requests it.

> ➤ **Discussion: What sort of organisation could use**
>
>   **(a) the first type of distributed database?**
>
>   **(b) the second type of database?**

Advantages and limitations of distributed databases

Distributed systems reduce the dependence on a single, massive central database. They increase responsiveness to local users' and customers' needs. They can provide a better response rate to queries which are handled locally.

Depending on how the distributed database is held, however, it can be highly dependent on powerful and reliable telecommunications systems. Local databases can sometimes depart from central data definitions and standards, and security can be compromised when distribution widens access to sensitive data.

Despite these drawbacks, distributed processing is growing rapidly. For large organisations operating on several sites, the question is not *whether* to distribute but *how* to distribute in order to minimise costs, increase efficiency and provide the best service while not compromising data integrity and security.

Using telecommunications for competitive advantage

The use of telecommunications is increasingly being used to reshape the way that organisations do business, increasing the efficiency and speed of operations, making management more effective and providing better services to customers. For example:

- A large publisher has a telecommunications link to its distributor's warehouse. Under the old system, when an order was received from a bookshop or wholesaler, invoices were printed and sent by post to the warehouse where one copy was sent with the box of books and a second copy retained for reference. Under the new system the invoice is transferred electronically and printed at the warehouse, enabling books to be shipped out at least 24 hours earlier.

- Amazon.com takes orders from customers over the Internet. Some core stock of popular items is held, but if the item is not in stock, an order to the supplier is then placed by Amazon electronically in a 'just-in-time' system and the CD or video normally shipped within 48 hours. Confirmation of the order is sent by e-mail to the customer, and in the case of delays, the customer can find out via the Internet where the order has got to.

- Yellow Pages has equipped its sales force with laptop computers from which they can initiate a phone call by clicking a phone number displayed in the database. Instead of faxing sales enquiries and mock-ups for advertisements, mobile staff can now access a fully automated sales system and query the corporate database direct. When an advertisement is approved, it can be sent from the salesperson's home computer to the production department at head office via ISDN.

- SMI, an advertising agency, uses a company-wide internal network (an 'Intranet') to share documents though a single viewing interface, Lotus Notes. Through a password-protected front end, customers can access and inspect prospective campaigns the moment they come off the digital drawing board, and comment on them, sending their text straight into SMI's Notes system. A proposed radio advertisement could be put on the system and a client in Timbuktu could listen to it a minute later.

Case study: United Parcel Service (UPS)

UPS is a major package delivery and shipping company which does a large part of its business over the Internet. When a manufacturer has products to sell to a customer, they use a service like UPS to deliver the goods.

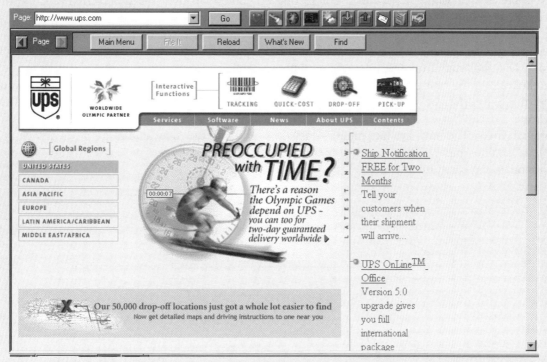

UPS uses a nationwide cellular system called TotalTrack to provide information at any time, day or night, on the status of a parcel. When the driver picks up a package, it is immediately logged using a portable hand-held computer containing a barcode reader for capturing the barcode identification on the package, and a keyboard for entering additional information such as the destination's area code. On returning to the truck, the driver inserts the hand-held computer into a small computer that transmits the data to the local dispatch centre, where it is recorded on a database. The location data is updated automatically as the package moves through each step on the way to its destination. The combination of telecommunications and computing permits UPS to know the location of every package at any time.

When the package is delivered to the customer, the customer signs for it using a pen-based computer and delivery confirmation is transmitted back to UPS.

Both sender and receiver of the package can track the status of the parcel at any time, day or night, via the Internet using UPS's OnLineTM Office software.

As UPS says: "After placing an order with you most customers have just one question on their minds: When will my shipment arrive? With just one click you can give them the answer! Just go to the UPS

OnLineTM Office software and click on Ship Notification. From there, you can send consignees a detailed fax report showing who sent the shipment, where the shipment was sent, and when it's scheduled for delivery. All with no phone calls to make and no calls to answer. There's just no easier way to keep customers satisfied.

> ➢ **Discussion: This is an example of a highly distributed system, with data about each parcel being held at local dispatch centres, accessible from all over the world. What are the advantages of this system to UPS, the consigner of the parcel, and the recipient?**

> ➢ **Apart from knowing where the parcel is, could UPS use this system to provide other services to its customers?**

The Internet and the World Wide Web

The Internet is a network of networks, connecting computers all over the globe. In 1969, the Internet started life as the ARPANET (Advanced Research Projects Agency Network) and consisted of just 4 computers. By the beginning of 1997, it included 1.7 million computers and it continues to grow exponentially. The cables, wires and satellites that carry Internet data form an interlinked communications network. Data traveling from one Internet computer to another is transmitted from one link in the network to another, along the best possible route. If some links are overloaded or out of service, the data can be routed through different links. The major Internet communications links are called the **Internet backbone**. A handful of network service providers (NSPs) such as BT each maintain a series of nationwide links. The links are like pipes – data flows through the pipes and large pipes can carry more data than smaller pipes. NSPs are continually adding new communications links to the backbone to accommodate increased Internet use.

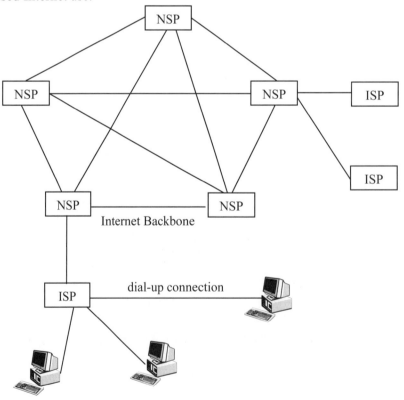

Figure 58.4: Structure of the Internet

320

When you connect your computer to the Internet, you do not connect directly to the backbone. Instead, you connect to an ISP (Internet Service Provider) that in turn connects to the backbone.

An ISP generally charges you a monthly fee for Internet access (though many such as Freeserve are free) and provides you with communications software and a user account. You need a computer with a modem to connect your computer to a phone line, and when you log on, your computer dials the ISP and establishes a connection over the phone line. Once you are connected, the ISP routes data between your computer and the Internet backbone. A phone line provides a very narrow pipe for transmitting data, having a typical capacity of 56 thousand bits per second. Using a phone line and a 56K modem, the time taken to transfer the contents of a 680Mb CD-ROM would be over 26 hours!

The World Wide Web is a special part of the Internet which allows people to view information stored on participating computers. It is an easy-to-use, graphical source of information which has opened the Internet to millions of people interested in finding out information. It consists of documents called pages that contain information on a particular topic, and links to other Web pages, which could be stored on other computers in different countries.

The role of servers and routers

Each individual network connected to the Internet has its own network server, on which data files are held. The files on each website on the World Wide Web are held on file servers belonging to different ISPs. When you log on to a website and download data, it is split up into small packets of data and transmitted from the ISP's server to your computer, or to your network server if you are connected to a network. The data packets may travel by different routes before being recombined in the right sequence on arrival at their destination.

A router is a computer which connects multiple networks. It does this by storing the addresses of all the networks it is able to communicate with, how to connect to them and the paths between them. Using a combination of the network and node address, it can work out the best route for data packets to travel between different computers (nodes) on the network. Routers can route packets of the same **protocol** (such as TCP/IP, see Chapter 60) over networks with different physical or logical organisation (such as Ethernet to token ring).

To connect two networks with different architectures and different protocols, a **gateway** is required.

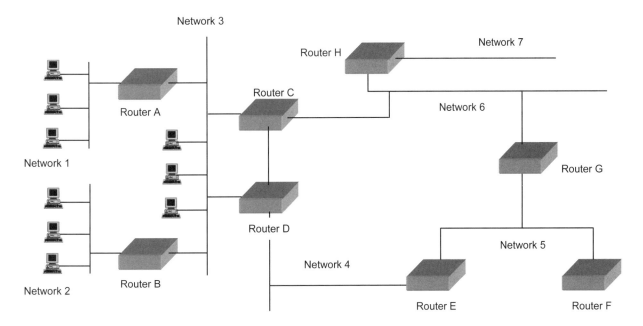

Figure 58.5: Routers provide alternative routes between networks

Exercises

1. (a) What is meant by distributed processing?   (2)
    (b) With the aid of an example, describe how distributed processing may be implemented in an
         organisation which has a Head Office, and several sites each with a number of different
         departments.   (5)

    New question

2. (a) Describe how a distributed database may be implemented.   (3)
    (b) Give an example of an organisation that might hold its data in this way.   (1)
    (c) What are the advantages and disadvantages of such a distributed database to this organisation?
                                                                                               (4)

    New question

3. A supermarket has direct links to some of its major suppliers so that orders can be sent electronically
    each day for 'just-in-time' delivery of goods that need replenishing. What are the advantages to
    (a) the supermarket
    (b) the suppliers
    of this arrangement   (4)

    New question

4. A large national charity holds a central database of donors and recipients. Branch offices equipped
    with PCs and modems are able to dial in over a telephone line to get lists of members living locally
    to inform them of local fund-raising events. What would be the advantages to the charity of a
    distributed system? How would distributed databases be kept in the same state as the central
    database?   (6)

    New question

5.

> Networks are the future!

    Explain why computer networking has developed rapidly over the past 15 years. Your answer should
    discuss **three** factors which have stimulated this development and **three** implications for society. (6)

    SEB Paper 2 Qu 10 1994

Chapter 59 – Network Security and Accounting

Introduction

Computer networks bring their own particular security problems. One of the great advantages of networks is that data held on databases can be accessed by people from all over the world – but clearly, this poses the threat that the data may be accessed, stolen, altered or deleted by unauthorised people – or even by authorised employees with criminal tendencies. Checking up on the honesty of prospective employees by taking up references before hiring them should be one of a company's most essential security policies.

In this chapter we'll look at methods used to help keep data held on networked computers secure, as far as possible. *(No system is completely foolproof!)*

Training users about security

Every employee should be made aware of the company's security policy and of the risks to data held on networks. The importance of following rules and procedures, and of being alert to possible breaches of security, need to be emphasised and understood. Downloading programs from the Internet, for example, can introduce viruses on to a computer network, and so all such files should be virus-checked before use. All employees should be made aware of their responsibilities not to allow strangers access to restricted areas, not to leave machines logged on while they go to lunch and not to write their password down.

Access privileges

The main method of controlling access to data held on a network is by defining **access privileges** for each user. These define for each user exactly which computers and what data he or she is allowed to access, and what they are allowed to do with data they can access. Typical access levels include:

- No access;
- Read only;
- Read and copy;
- Read and update.

Junior nursing staff, for example, might be able to access a patient's medical record in a hospital but not to update it. A doctor from another hospital might be able to read and copy it, and the patient's own doctor would be able to read and update the record.

Access controls can be applied to software as well as data, so that users have access to software needed for their particular tasks, but not to other software.

Access control

Access control may be based on:

- **What you know** – for example a password or PIN number. These suffer from many shortcomings, as users tend to be careless about using obvious words or names, or writing their passwords down. Many computer system break-ins occur because a password has been divulged to someone who appeared to be authorised to know it – for example a repairman. The fraudster can, for example, run a program which appears to be a login procedure but which simply writes a password to a file. The unsuspecting user is then requested to type in their password as part of the 'repair'.

- **What you have** – for example, an ID card perhaps in the form of a smart card or magnetic stripe card.

- **Where you are** – you may be able to gain entry to a computer system only from a specified location or telephone number. Using a **callback system**, the user dials in and enters an ID number and password, and is then automatically disconnected. The computer checks the ID and password and if these are correct, the user is called back at a predetermined telephone number.

- **Who you are** – specialised equipment can check your handprint, retinal image or voice print. These are all forms of **biometric identification**.

All these methods of identifying authorised users can be made less effective if users are careless about leaving terminals unattended when they are logged on. Some systems automatically log off if there is no activity at a terminal for a specified period, say 10 minutes.

Firewalls

Linking to the Internet or transmitting information via Intranets requires special security measures. A **firewall** is software that prevents unauthorised communication into or out of the network, allowing the organisation to enforce a security policy on traffic flowing between its network and the Internet. The firewall is generally placed between internal LANs and WANs and external networks such as the Internet.

Various different types of firewall products are available, such as:

- A router which examines each incoming packet of data, checking its source or destination address. Access rules must identify every type of packet that the organisation does not want to admit;

- Special software that restricts traffic to a particular application such as e-mail or Lotus Notes groupware;

- A 'proxy server' that maintains replicated copies of Web pages for easy access by a designated class of users. Outside visitors to the Web site can be routed to this information while being denied access to more sensitive information.

Audit controls

Audit controls track all activity on a network – for example:

- What programs have been used;
- What files have been opened;
- How many reads and writes have been executed;
- How many times a server has been accessed.

Special monitoring software can also be used to produce statistical profiles and store statistics about the behaviour of each user with respect to objects such as data files or programs. The program can then detect statistically abnormal behaviour of users.

Performance management

Network monitoring software will collect data and statistics on all aspects of network use to help with the management and planning of a network. Data may be collected on:

- Network availability (i.e. switched on and not working);
- Response time (time between making a query and receiving a response);
- Utilisation of hardware resources (CPU, disks, bridges, repeaters, clients and servers);
- Utilisation of software;
- Traffic density in each segment of a network.

These statistics can help to identify bottlenecks and potential problems and aid in planning future developments. By monitoring software usage, it is possible to detect if there are more copies of any particular software package being used than the company has a licence for, and take action.

> ➤ **Discussion: What action should the Computer Centre management take if it detects illegal use of software?**
>
> ➤ **In what other ways could it be useful to monitor software usage?**

Data encryption

Data on a network is vulnerable to wire-tapping when it is being transmitted over a network, and one method of preventing confidential data from being read by unauthorised hackers is to **encrypt** it, making it incomprehensible to anyone who does not hold the 'key' to decode it.

There are many ways of encrypting data, often based on either **transposition** (where characters are switched around) or substitution (where characters are replaced by other characters).

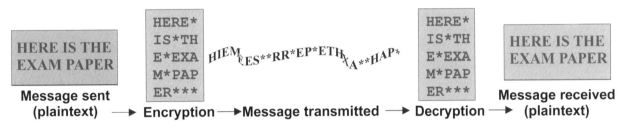

Figure 59.1: Data encryption

In a **transposition** cipher, the message could be written in a grid row by row and transmitted column by column. The sentence 'Here is the exam paper' could be written in a 5 x 5 grid:

```
H E R E *
I S * T H
E * E X A
M * P A P
E R * * *
```

And transmitted as HIEMEES**RR*EP*ETHXA**HAP*

> ➤ **Using the same grid, decode the message ITT*O*E*HRWDNIYA*OS*NITT***

Using a substitution cipher, a 'key' that is known to both sender and receiver is used to code the message. A very simple example is to substitute each letter with the next one in the alphabet.

In practice, since the key must be difficult to break, a much more sophisticated algorithm must be used, with frequent changes of key.

Cryptography serves three purposes:

• It helps to identify authentic users ;

• It prevents alteration of the message;

• It prevents unauthorised users from reading the message.

Accounting software

Accounting software may be used to monitor and charge users for network use. The charge may depend on:

- Amount of time logged on;
- Processing time;
- Resources used (such as disk space or printer);
- Time of day, with peak periods attracting a higher charge.

Like auditing software, accounting software may also be used to monitor the pattern of usage, so that for example users can be encouraged to make use of less busy times during the day. The monitoring process can help network administrators to decide when upgrades or new resources such as extra colour printers are required.

Exercises

1. A university provides staff and students with access to its computer network.

    (a) Activity on the university's networking system is monitored and an accounting log is automatically produced. Suggest what this log might include and explain why it is useful.   (8)

    (b) Appropriate staff have access to personal and financial data. What steps should be taken to preserve the security of the data in such a system?   (4)

    NEAB IT05 Qu 4 1997

2. One method of encryption used in transmitting data requires data to be placed in a grid with 4 rows and 5 columns. The data enters row by row and is transmitted column by column.

    (a) Show that the data string "THE*EXAM*BEGINS*AT*9" would be sent as

    "TXE*HAGAEMIT**N*EBS9"

    (b) Decode the following received message using the same grid, showing how you obtain your answer.

    "TIS*HSSFI*AOSMGU*EER"   (4)

    London Computing Paper 1 Qu 2 1996

3. The IT manager of a large college is about to change the software that is used to record student attendance in classes. Given that this new software must provide different access permissions and types of report, what capabilities and restrictions should the IT manager allocate in order to satisfy the needs of each of the following groups of users?

    - students
    - teaching staff
    - office staff
    - senior managers   (8)

    NEAB IT05 Qu 4 1999

4. Whilst planning to install a network accounting system, a company has become concerned about the security of its local computer network.

    (a) Explain **two** procedures that the company could adopt to discourage breaches of security.   (6)

    (b) State **two** reasons for using accounting software on a network.   (2)

    AQA ICT5 Qu 5 January 2003

Chapter 60 – Data Communications and Standards

Communications software

Communications software enables computers to communicate with each other, controlling transmission by specifying, for example:

- **Speed of transmission**. This will depend on whether a baseband or broadband line is being used, and the speed of the modem.

- **Method of transmission** – for example, serial or parallel transmission

- **Which computer code is used** (e.g. ASCII, EBCDIC)

- **Type of parity used** (e.g. odd or even).

The rules and procedures for allowing computers to communicate with each other is called the **communications protocol**.

Speed of transmission

Transmission speed is related to the bandwidth of the communications channel. A communications 'channel' is the link between two computers and could be, for example, a telephone line, a fibre-optic or coaxial cable, a microwave or satellite link.

There are two common types of bandwidth called *baseband* and *broadband*.

- **Baseband** carries one signal at a time. A bit value of 0 or 1 is sent by the presence or absence of a voltage in the cable. Baseband signals can travel very fast but can only be sent over short distances. Over about 1000 feet special booster equipment is needed.

- **Broadband** can carry multiple signals on a fixed carrier wave, with the signals for 0 and 1 sent as variations on this wave. Data, audio and video transmission can take place simultaneously.

The speed at which data is sent is expressed as the baud rate, measured in bits per second (bps). The computer code for a single character typically uses 7 or 8 bits, and in addition a start and stop bit and/or a parity bit is added to this, so that each character requires say 10 bits. Thus a speed of 56,000bps means that about 5,600 characters a second can be transmitted.

Modems

Telephone lines were originally designed for speech, which is transmitted in analogue or wave form. In order for digital data to be sent along a telephone line, it must first be converted to analogue form and then converted back at the other end, hence the need for a MOdulator/DEModulator. Modems typically transmit data at rates of between 9,600 and 56,600bps.

Figure 60.1: Modem

Serial and parallel transmission

In serial transmission, each bit is transmitted one at a time over a single channel. There are two types of serial mode for sending data – synchronous and asynchronous. In asynchronous transmission, one character at a time is transmitted, with a start and stop bit sent with each character. This is generally used for lower speed transmission, for example on a local area network. Synchronous transmission enables whole blocks of data to be sent in timed sequences, and is much faster.

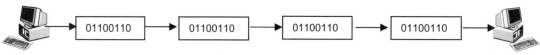

Figure 60.2: Serial transmission

In parallel transmission, all the bits making up a character, together with a parity bit (if used) are transmitted simultaneously. Parallel transmission is limited to communications over short distances of a few metres, for example between a computer and a printer.

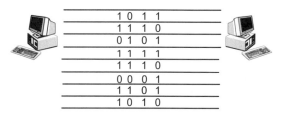

Figure 60.3: Parallel transmission

Telecommunications standards and protocols

In order to allow machines from different manufacturers to communicate with each other over local or wide area networks, standards covering all aspects of communication from the number of pins on connectors to how a particular software package displays a menu at a user's terminal need to be defined.

Although having standards makes it possible to create networks containing hardware from different vendors (such as Apple and IBM), there are tradeoffs. Standards may disallow certain features or capabilities that are valuable in a particular situation but inconsistent with the standard. Standards may also prohibit features which certain vendors have built into their hardware in order to steal a march on the competition – something that is better than other architectures but will not work with other hardware. In spite of this, most people would rather have hardware that has less than the maximum capabilities but is compatible with their other hardware, and welcome the introduction of standards.

Standards can be divided into *de facto* standards and *de jure* standards. **De facto standards** are established by the fact that a particular product dominates the market, like Intel microprocessors or Microsoft's products. **De jure standards** are defined by industry groups or by government.

The **OSI** (Open System Interface) was created to guide the development of standards for communications between networked systems, regardless of technology, vendor or country of origin. The standards have been developed by an industry consortium called the International Standards Organisation, and they cover all aspects of network operations and management.

Other standards and protocols such as IBM's Systems Network Architecture, and standards set up by other manufacturers, exist but there is a strong desire to have just one international standard which will provide a seamless system of communication between any type of network. The OSI model protocol will be the principal means of ensuring this.

The development of de facto standards

Some technologies don't depend on widespread acceptance for their value. A device that automatically opens a garage door when you point at it and press a button may be very useful even if you're the only person in the world who has one. But for products that depend on communications or collaboration between different organisations, much of a product's value comes from its widespread acceptance. There is no point owning a new type of CD player that plays full-length videos on a TV screen, if no one has recorded the videos that you want to watch. Likewise, there is no point buying a computer that is much faster than any other, and has a better user interface, unless it will run the software that you want to use. You're better off with the slower one that will do the job.

> ➤ **Discussion: Why do all keyboards have the same layout of letters, i.e. QWERTY along the top line? Would it be a good idea to adopt a new standard?**
>
> ➤ **In England we push a light switch down to turn the light on. In the US, 'Up' is On. These are 'de facto' standards – standards that have evolved.**
>
> ➤ **Think of some 'de facto' standards applicable to PCs.**

De facto standards are developed by the marketplace rather than by law.

Case study: Microsoft's MS-DOS

In the summer of 1980 two emissaries from IBM came to Microsoft – then a tiny, unknown company – to discuss a personal computer they said IBM might or might not build. Working with the IBM design team Microsoft encouraged IBM to build one of the first computers to use the 16-bit microprocessor chip, the Intel 8088. The move from 8 bits to 16 bits meant that the PC would be able to support up to one full megabyte of memory – 256 times as much as an 8-bit computer. Microsoft granted IBM the royalty-free right to use their MS-DOS operating system for a one-time fee of about $80,000. In other words, they practically gave it away – but their goal was not to make money from IBM but to license the operating system software to other companies who made IBM-compatible machines.

Consumers bought the IBM PC with confidence, and by 1982 third party software developers began turning out applications to run on it. Each new customer and each new application added to the IBM PC's strength as a de facto standard for the industry, until almost all of the newest and best software was written for PCs running MS-DOS. A positive-feedback cycle began to drive the PC market, so that within three years, almost all other personal computers (Apple being the main exception) had disappeared. Many new companies such as Eagle and Northstar (ever heard of them?) thought people would buy their new computers because they offered something different and slightly better than the IBM PC. They were wrong. The IBM PC had become the hardware standard.

Internet protocol

Communication between computers connected to the Internet is governed by a protocol named TCP/IP (Transport Control Protocol/Internet Protocol), which has become a *de facto* standard. By following this standard set of communications rules, Internet computers can efficiently control and route data between your computer and the Internet computers maintained by ISPs and NSPs.

Addressing mechanisms on the World Wide Web

Every host computer (e.g. Internet Service Provider) connected to the Internet has a unique IP (Internet Protocol) address. This is a collection of four numbers separated by full stops, (e.g. 123.012.219.152). There are plans to extend and expand this system since the net will shortly run out of available addresses.

As these numbers are impossible to memorise, the **Domain Name System** translates these numbers into a domain name which identifies the organisation and often the country in which the computer is located (e.g. amazon.com, guardian.co.uk).

A **URL** (Uniform Resource Locator) is the standard address used to find a page, Web server or other device on the Web or the Internet. A Web site has a Home Page and usually links to several other pages on the site. Each page has its own unique case-sensitive URL.

For example, the Payne-Gallway Web site home page has the address

http://www.payne-gallway.co.uk/

The first part of the address (http://)

specifies the protocol used for connection to the server. http stands for Hypertext Transfer Protocol, which is used for Web sites. Other kinds of protocols include

https://   'Hypertext Transfer Protocol, Secure' for a Web site with security features. Credit card numbers should be safer here.

ftp://   'File Transfer Protocol' for an FTP site. FTP software allows you to upload and download files to and from computers throughout the world.

The second part of the address (www)

indicates which part of the Internet is being addressed, in this case the World Wide Web.

The third part of the address (payne-gallway)

is the first part of the **domain name**, called the 'sub-domain'. This comprises the name of the institution or people running the site or the computer which it is stored on, for example *payne-gallway*.

The fourth part of the address (.co)

is known as the 'top level domain'. It tells you what sort of institution is behind the site. For example:

.ac or .edu	an academic institution
.co	a company that trades in a single country
.com	a commercial organisation that trades internationally
.gov	a government department or other related facility
.org	a non-commercial organisation such as a charity
.sch	a school (this code is specific to the UK)

Some additional domains are:

.plc or .ltd	for companies
.biz	for businesses
.net	for entities emphasizing activities related to the Internet
.tv	for entities to do with television

.info   for entities providing information services

.me   for those wishing individual or personal nomenclature

The fifth part of the address (.uk)

specifies the country in which the site is located, .jp for Japan, .de for Germany, .es for Spain, .ie for Ireland, .sg for Singapore, etc.

Note that a URL, like a domain name, is an Internet address. A URL is the address of a *document* on the computer, whereas a domain name represents the IP address of a *computer*.

Each page at a website is a file with the extension .htm or html, written in HTML (Hypertext Markup Language). If you click on the catalogue link on the payne-gallway site, for example, you will be taken to another page with a URL http://www.payne-gallway.co.uk/catalogue.html

To find out more about domain names – how to register them, how to sell them, who runs them etc., try either of the following sites: http://www.igoldrush.com or http://www.netnames.co.uk. The first is a very informative, clear and entertaining guide to the whole business of domain names and well worth a visit. The second is less funky but gives plenty of information, useful especially if you want to register a domain name of your own.

Exercises

1. (a) What is meant by the term wide area network?   (1)
    (b) Explain the term protocol in the context of transmission over a wide area network. (2)
    (c) Why is a protocol needed for a wide area network?   (1)
                                                              AEB Computing Paper 3 Qu 2 1999

2. Explain what is meant by the terms
    IP (Internet Protocol) address, domain name, URL (Uniform Resource Locator).   (3)
                                                                           New question

3. Networks of computers are rapidly becoming part of everyday life, both for organisations and individuals. Communication over networks involves the use of protocols.
    (a) Define the term *protocol.*   (1)
    (b) With the aid of an example, describe **one** advantage of using protocols.   (3)
    (c) State **one** consideration that should be taken into account when setting up a network, and explain why it is important.   (2)
                                                                  AQA ICT5 Qu 3 June 2002

4. (a) Describe what is meant by *de facto* standards. Give an example.   (3)
    (b) Describe one other way in which standards can be set in the ICT industry. Give an example. (3)
                                                                           New question

Chapter 61 – Human-Computer Interaction

Computers in the workplace

'Ergonomics' – the design and functionality of the environment – was discussed briefly in Chapter 13 (Health and Safety). Applying ergonomics successfully means studying the whole office environment to see how it can be made into a comfortable, safe and productive place in which to work. To begin with, simple measures such as persuading staff to tidy their desks or reorganise the office furniture so that people are not in danger of tripping over telephone and computer cables can achieve a great deal.

Lighting should be carefully chosen so that the office is neither overlit nor underlit, avoiding excessive contrast between lit and unlit areas, or patches of shadow falling on work areas. Computers should not face windows, as the glare will be unbearable, and nor should users be forced to sit facing a window with the sun in their eyes. The optimal position for computer monitors is side on to a window. Windows should have adjustable blinds so that the changing light from the sun can be controlled.

Furniture must be comfortable and adjustable. Poorly-designed chairs are responsible for back trouble, and chairs at the wrong height can contribute to the onset of repetitive strain injury (RSI), an affliction which affects people who spend too many hours at a keyboard without breaks and in uncomfortable positions. Short people may need a footrest, and are now legally entitled to ask for one.

Environmental considerations have led to more manufacturers producing energy-efficient computer systems. It is estimated that the electricity used by computers accounts for between 5 and 10% of the USA's annual total commercial electricity bill. Research suggests that computers are used for only a tiny proportion of the time that they are switched on, with over a quarter of the nation's computers running overnight and at weekends. Energy-efficient computers and printers which go into 'sleep' mode, a low-power state, when the unit is inactive, stand to save US businesses $2 billion per year. Apart from the money, the use of energy-efficient products will reduce emission of carbon dioxide by 20 million tonnes, roughly comparable to the emissions of 5 million cars.

Psychological factors

Apart from the physical factors, there are numerous psychological factors which affect our interaction with computers. An understanding of how we receive, process and store information can be used to design effective, user-friendly interactive systems.

Information is received through senses, and a knowledge of human senses and skills is used by interface designers.

- **Vision.** Research has shown, for example, that the eye is less sensitive to blue light than to red or green, and therefore important information should not be displayed in blue text. Also, 8% of males and 1% of females are colour-blind, most commonly being unable to distinguish between red and green. Therefore, no interface should depend on everyone being able to distinguish colours.

- **Hearing.** Sound is commonly used for warning sounds in interfaces, for example to tell the user that they have tried to perform an illegal operation – humans can distinguish between a wide range of sounds and can react faster to auditory stimuli than to visual ones. The SonicFinder for the Macintosh uses auditory icons to represent desktop objects and actions. Copying is indicated by the sound of pouring liquid into a bottle. A file arriving in a mailbox sounds like a large parcel if it is very large, or a light packet if it is small.

- **Touch**. Touch is an important in keyboard and mouse design. The feeling of a button being depressed is an important part of the task of pressing it.
- **Movement**. Speed and accuracy are measures of motor skills and are important considerations in interface design. Users may find it difficult to manipulate small objects and so targets should generally be reasonably large.

Short-term memory

We have two main types of memory: short-term memory and long-term memory. Short-term memory is used for example to remember a telephone number for the length of time it takes to dial it after looking it up. The average person can remember 7 plus or minus 2 digits. Look at the number sequence

472081325

Now write it down. Did you get it right? Now try the sequence

649 723 106

Grouping the digits can increase short-term memory. It is also much easier to remember information that you can find a pattern in. For example, you probably won't be able to remember the sequence of letters

AST NIG HTW EWE NTT OTH ECI NEM AL

However, if you notice that by moving the last character to the first position, you will get a sentence by reblocking the letters into words instead of groups of three, you should have no trouble in being able to reproduce the letters.

Long-term memory

Long-term memory is used for the long-term storage of information – factual information, experiential knowledge and 'rules' about behaviour and procedures are stored here. It differs from short-term memory in a number of respects. Firstly, it has an almost limitless capacity. Secondly, it has a relatively slow access time of approximately a tenth of a second. Thirdly, forgetting occurs much more slowly in long-term memory.

Information can be moved from short-term memory to long-term memory by rehearsal or repetition. In addition, information is easier to remember if it is meaningful. Thus, it is difficult to remember a series of unconnected words such as

Violet hope see gannet builder green yesterday new sadly may

but much easier to memorise a sentence such as

I'll have a crocodile sandwich and make it snappy.

In other words, learning is aided by structure and familiarity.

We all carry around with us a mental picture of how the world works, put together from experiences stored in long-term memory. Consider the sentences:

Richard took his cat to the surgery. After seeing the vet he took the cat home.

You will probably assume from this that Richard consulted the vet, the cat was treated, Richard paid the bill and they left – rather than assuming that Richard took one look at the vet and took the cat home immediately.

Principles and results from research in psychology have been distilled into guidelines for designing user interfaces.

> ➢ **Discussion: One guiding principle for interface design is that you should never use an image which contradicts our mental image of how things are – for example, Red means Stop, Green means Go. Can you think of other examples?**

Designing good software

Interacting with computers can be a daunting, frightening and incomprehensible business to novices, and on occasion an infuriating experience for experts. Repeated failure with a new software package is frustrating and depressing and soon becomes boring. Researchers into human-computer interaction (HCI) study good software design to see what makes it good, and observe people interacting with computers to find out what they find easy, and which parts of the software lead them to make more errors than necessary, or what difficulties they encounter.

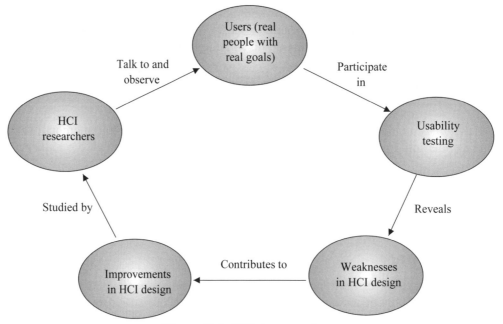

Figure 61.1: HCI design cycle

The best user interfaces provide:

- Help for novice users;
- Short cuts for experts;
- 'Metaphors' or images which are meaningful, such as the letter *W* on the icon for Word, or a picture of a printer for a print tool;
- Consistent behaviour which makes use of long-term memory, such as always using the function key F1 for Help, or the Escape key to get out of trouble;
- Clear, helpful error messages;
- Uncluttered screens with effective use of colour, with text that is easy to read.

Text versus graphics

The graphical user interface is appealing and generally far easier to use than a command interface, but sometimes icons cannot express an abstract concept and menus of one kind or another are essential.

Specialist products such as a travel agent's package may use a command interface in preference to a GUI because graphical interfaces generally:

- Occupy more memory;
- Need more space on disk;
- Run more slowly if complex graphics and many windows are open;
- Can be more time-consuming for an experienced operator than simply typing in a command.

Exercises

1. A new shopping centre requires a computerised interactive information system. The system is to have a number of information points distributed throughout the centre. The diagram below shows a plan of the centre.

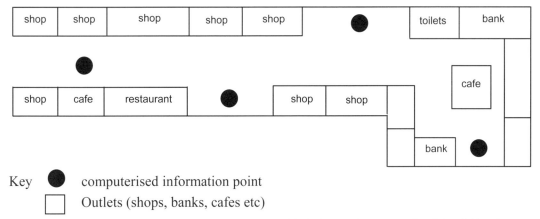

Key   ●   computerised information point

        □   Outlets (shops, banks, cafes etc)

The computerised information points have to provide information on each of the following:

Shops; Restaurants; Toilets; Disabled facilities; Advertising; A map of the centre; Banking services.

(a) The system has to have a suitable user interface.

Describe aspects which should be considered when designing the user interface. (4)

(b) Individual outlets will have the facility to use the system to provide up-to-the-minute details of special offers, opening hours, etc.

Describe the hardware and software that would be necessary to implement this facility. (3)

SEB Paper 1 Qu 11 1995

2. (a) Give **six** of the physical and psychological factors which govern how people interact with computer systems. (6)

(b) Give **three** factors which should be considered when providing a sophisticated human-computer interface, explaining the impact of each one on the system's resources. (6)

NEAB IT05 Qu 7 1997

3. (a) What are the factors you need to take into account when designing a screen layout for a database application? (6)

(b) What are the resource implications for providing a sophisticated human/computer interface? (4)

NEAB IT05 Qu 9 Sample Paper

4. A mail order company has decided to expand and has established a retail outlet in a busy shopping centre.

(a) An important feature of the mail order system is the interface for the staff who use it.

State **three** features you would expect the human/computer interface to have in such a system and give a different reason for each one. (6)

(b) (i) Name an appropriate device for capturing data on each item that is sold via the retail outlet. (1)

(ii) Describe **one** advantage for the company of using this device. (2)

AQA ICT5 Qu 8 January 2003

Chapter 62 – Software Acquisition and Testing

Make or buy?

At the start of the systems life cycle, a new computer project is proposed and a feasibility study is carried out to examine the economic, technical and social feasibility of the project. If a decision is made to go ahead, one of the major decisions that will have to be made is how to acquire the software. There are several options:

- The software may be written by the end-user;

- A specialist department within the organisation may design, write, test and document the software;

- External consultants may be called in to write and test the software;

- An off-the-shelf package may be bought, and possibly customised;

- Software may be leased rather than purchased, with the user paying an annual fee for the right to use the product.

End-user-written software

This is normally only an option for a very small project where the end-user is perhaps a computer specialist in their own right. A computer-literate enthusiast in a Recruitment Department, for example, may use a database package such as Access to write an application to input and analyse information about prospective or new recruits to help plan future advertising campaigns.

The advantages of the end-user writing the software is that the requirements are precisely known so no problems of communication arise, and the software is likely to be developed quite quickly in response to a specific need. The disadvantages are that the end-user is very unlikely to provide any technical or user documentation so that when he or she leaves, the software will probably quickly fall into disuse.

This option is only useful for minor projects with a limited life-span.

> ➢ **Discussion: Fifteen or so years ago it was quite common for, say, an enthusiastic doctor at a GP's surgery to buy a PC and develop his own software for an application such as printing out repeat prescriptions. Does this still happen? If not, why not?**

Writing software in-house

Many large organisations have their own department of computer specialists for maintaining existing software and developing new software. It is estimated that as much as 75% of computer specialists' time may be spent on maintenance – keeping existing programs running and making changes to them as required. Any opportunity to participate in a new project is likely to be received enthusiastically. This approach also has the advantage that any confidential information or ideas are kept within the organisation and will not be given to competitors by outside consultants.

However, developing a major new system may require extra staff with specialised skills and such people may be difficult to recruit, especially if they are only needed for a relatively short time. The company may decide it is preferable to bring in outside consultants who have the necessary experience and expertise.

External consultants

For a major project, going to an external software house may be the only solution. The job may be 'put out to tender', with several companies submitting proposals and being invited to give presentations of their proposals before one is chosen. The more complex the project, the greater the pitfalls, and so great care is needed in the choice of consultant. Cost is always a consideration but a consultant who can point to several successful systems already installed may be worth the extra money. The relationship that a consultant builds with the client may be one of the most important factors in implementing a new system successfully.

> ➤ **Discussion: What criteria would you use in deciding between several external consultants who had submitted proposals for delivering a new system?**

Buying a package

If a package is available to do the job, this may be a very safe and relatively inexpensive way to acquire the new software. A package has the following advantages over specially written software:

- It is cheaper than custom-written software – the development costs of the package may be millions of pounds, but the customer may be able to buy it for a few hundred pounds, since sales are made to thousands of other customers;
- It is immediately available and already thoroughly tested so is unlikely to have major bugs in it;
- Documentation is usually available in the form of reference manuals, user guides and tutorials;
- Training courses may be available from third-party trainers;
- Technical support is usually available from the manufacturers via a Web site or telephone line (at a price);
- Other users of the package can be consulted as to its suitability before purchase;
- Upgrades are usually available every year or two.

Disadvantages of a package solution include:

- The package may not do exactly what you want it to do;
- It may not run on the firm's existing hardware;
- It may not interface with other software already in use in the organisation.

Leasing software

Some packages are leased rather than purchased. This means that the user will automatically receive regular upgrades, and the initial expense is less. In the long run, of course, this option may be more expensive.

Modifying existing packages

Sometimes a package is bought and modified. This is in general a very dangerous option as it means that the manufacturer will no longer provide any technical support, and the modifications are likely to cause errors in other parts of the software, which therefore require more modifications, and so on.

Criteria for selecting a software solution

When a company decides it needs to purchase new software for a particular purpose, it will need to evaluate different packages based on specific criteria. These criteria may be different according to the type of software being purchased. For example, suppose a doctors' surgery is considering buying a new package to hold patient records and keep track of appointments.

It may use the following criteria in assessing each software package under consideration:

- Functionality – it must be able to do all the required tasks such as storing patient records and allowing patient appointments to be logged. It must be multi-user to enable several doctors and receptionists to use it simultaneously.

- Robustness – the program must be error-free and handle large amounts of data without crashing.

- Performance – the software must handle requests for data and other functions quickly so that the users do not have to wait while the computer finds patient data or the right day for booking an appointment.

- Support – users will require some initial training in the package, and they will need access to someone who can help when problems are encountered.

- Portability – it may be necessary to use data for statistical analyses or for a mail merge to selected patients so it is essential that data can be exported to different packages such as Excel, Access or Word.

- Transferability – if the surgery already has a lot of patient data stored on computer, then it must be possible to transfer all this data to the new system without the need for re-keying.

- Appropriateness – it must be straightforward for doctors, nurses and receptionists to use in different ways. It should cater for different levels of computer literacy.

- Security – it should have features built in to ensure that patient data is kept secure and is accessible only to authorised employees.

- Upgradability – the package will be in use for a long time and the surgery will need to look to the future and make sure that it will be possible to purchase upgrades as required.

> ➤ **Discussion: Imagine that a local newsagent is planning to buy a new software package to help with the running of the store. What criteria will he apply in assessing each new package? Why is each of these criteria important?**

Software testing

All software has to undergo a rigorous testing process before it can be released. When a new system is developed, the testing process may typically consist of five stages:

1. **Unit testing.** Each individual component (such as a subroutine or code for a particular function) of the new system is tested.
2. **Module testing.** A module is defined in this context as a collection of dependent components or subroutines.
3. **Subsystem testing.** This phase involves testing collections of modules which have been integrated into subsystems. (For example, the Purchase Order function may be one of the subsystems of an Accounting system.) Subsystems are often independently designed and programmed and problems can arise owing to interface mismatches. Therefore, these interfaces need to be thoroughly tested.

4. **System testing**. The subsystems are integrated to make up the entire system. The testing may reveal errors resulting from the interaction between different subsystems. This stage of testing is also concerned with ensuring that the system meets all the requirements of the original specification.

5. **Acceptance testing**. This is the final stage in the testing process before the system is accepted for operational use. It involves testing the system with data supplied by the system purchaser rather than with simulated data developed specially for testing purposes.

Testing is an iterative process, with each stage in the test process being repeated when modifications have to be made owing to errors coming to light at a subsequent stage.

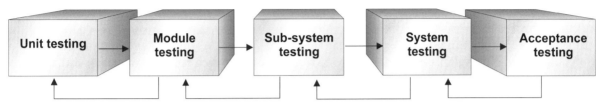

Figure 62.1: Stages in testing new software

Alpha testing

Acceptance testing is sometimes known as **alpha testing**. For specially commissioned software, this testing continues until agreement is reached between the developer and the system purchaser that the system works correctly and fulfils all the system requirements.

Alpha testing is essential because it often reveals both errors and omissions in the system requirements definition. The user may discover that the system does not in fact have the required functionality because the requirements were not specified carefully enough, or because the developer has overlooked or misunderstood something in the specification.

Beta testing

When a new package is being developed for release as a software package, beta testing is often used. This involves giving the package to a number of potential users who agree to use the system and report any problems to the developers. Microsoft, for example, deliver beta versions of their products to hundreds of sites for testing. This exposes the product to real use and detects problems and errors that may not have been anticipated by the developers. The product can then be modified and sent out for further beta testing until the developer is confident enough in the product to put it on the market.

Failure of software testing

The more complex a software package is, the harder it is to make sure that it contains no errors. If you have written any software yourself you will be aware of just how long it takes to test every aspect of even a simple software application. In practice almost all software contains some errors, and this may be due to factors such as the following.

- A desire to be first on to the market with a particular product may lead to cutting corners on testing.

- There may be a deadline by which the software is required, and so testing is not as thorough as it should be.

- The test plan or test data may be inadequate and some aspects of the software are not tested at all.

- The user may use the software in a manner which had not been anticipated by the developers, and which was therefore not tested.

Software maintenance

It is impossible to produce software which does not need to be maintained. Over the lifetime of any software system or package, maintenance will be required for a number of reasons:

- Errors may be discovered in the software;
- The original requirements are modified to reflect changing needs;
- Hardware developments may give scope for advances in software;
- New legislation may be introduced which impacts upon software systems (e.g. the introduction of a new tax).

Maintenance falls into three categories:

- **Perfective maintenance**. The system can be made better in some way without changing its functionality. For example it could be made to run faster or produce reports in a clearer format.

- **Adaptive maintenance**. Changing needs in a company may mean systems need to be adapted – for example, a single-user system may be adapted to a multi-user system. A new operating system or new hardware may also necessitate adaptive maintenance.

- **Corrective maintenance**. This involves the correction of previously undetected errors. Systems may appear to work correctly for some time before errors are discovered. Many commercial software programs such as Windows, Word or Access have bugs in them and maintenance releases are regularly brought out.

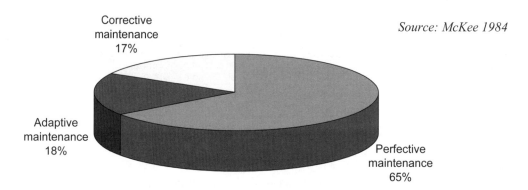

Source: McKee 1984

Figure 62.2: Maintenance effort distribution

Maintenance releases

The maintenance process is generally triggered by requests for changes from system users or by management. The costs and impacts of these changes is assessed and if the decision is made to go ahead with the proposed changes, a new release of the system is planned. The release will very likely involve elements of adaptive, corrective and perfective maintenance. The changes are implemented and tested and then a new version of the software is released.

Minor changes in software packages are often released with version numbers like Version 3.0, 3.1, etc. Major new releases may be given numbers like version 4.0, 5.0 etc., or a completely new name.

If purchasers of a new software package report a particular error, the manufacturer may produce a software 'patch' which can be downloaded from their website on the Internet. This is a temporary solution until a new version of the software is released.

Maintenance is often perceived by software developers as a rather inferior type of activity, requiring less skill than developing new software, and is therefore allocated to less experienced staff. This is probably one reason why such a high proportion of software costs are attributed to maintenance.

A study by Lehman and Belady carried out in 1985 resulted in a set of 'laws' of software maintenance.

---

1. **The law of continuing change**

   A program that is used in a real-world environment necessarily must change or become progressively less useful in that environment.

2. **The law of increasing complexity**

   As an evolving program changes, its structure tends to become more complex. Extra resources must be devoted to preserving and simplifying the structure.

3. **The law of large program evolution**

   Program evolution is a self-regulating process. System attributes such as size, time between releases and the number of reported errors are approximately invariant for each system release.

4. **The law of organisational stability**

   Over a program's lifetime, its rate of development is approximately constant and independent of the resources devoted to system development.

5. **The law of conservation of familiarity**

   Over the lifetime of a system, the incremental change in each release is approximately constant.

The third law above suggests that large systems have a dynamic of their own. Maintenance teams cannot simply make any changes they want to, because of structural and organisational factors. As changes are made to a system, new errors are introduced which then necessitate more changes. Major changes tend to be inhibited because these changes would be expensive and may result in a less reliable system. The number of changes which may be implemented at any one time is limited.

Maintenance is very expensive, being by far the greatest cost incurred in the overall systems life cycle. It is therefore cost-effective to put time and effort into developing systems which are as easy as possible to maintain.

Exercises

1. Before releasing a new package the software company carries out alpha and beta testing.
   (a) What are these two types of testing and why are they both needed? (6)
   (b) Explain why, once the package has been released, there may be a need for maintenance releases and how these might be dealt with. (6)

   NEAB IT05 Qu 8 Sample Paper

2. An examination board is considering developing a system which is to be used for maintaining and processing module test results of candidates.
   - Describe the different ways in which the examination board may be able to provide a software solution.
   - Discuss the issues the examination board should consider before choosing any particular solution. (20)

   NEAB IT05 Qu 9 1997

3. A large market research company is considering several different software packages to assist with the analysis of data collected on behalf of clients.

   Give **three** criteria that should be considered when evaluating these software packages. For each criterion, explain why it may be important to this company. (9)

   AQA ICT5 Qu 4 June 2002

ICT5 – Sample Questions and Answers

1. A manager has upgraded his desktop computer to take advantage of his company network environment.

   State **two** changes that you would expect him to see as a result of such an upgrade. (2)

   NEAB IT05 Qu 1 1999

Notes:

A bit of a trick question this, since you will get absolutely no marks for saying 'his applications will run faster' or ' he will be able to run the latest version of Microsoft Office'. The point is, he may not have changed his actual hardware, he's just had a network card installed, the sneaky so-and-so. Let this be a lesson to you. READ THE QUESTION CAREFULLY.

Suggested answer:

He will have an additional dialogue to deal with log-on, possibly including an ID and password.

He will be able to access files either on the server or on the other computers in the network, if it is a peer-to-peer network.

(Could also say, he will be able to use resources such as printers on the network.)

---

2. 'I don't care which version of a word-processing package the rest of the company uses. As a senior company manager I intend to upgrade my department to the latest version.' Give **four** potential problems this attitude may cause for other IT users in the company. (4)

   NEAB IT05 Qu 2 1998

Notes:

You have probably encountered problems with transferring documents written in one version of a software package between home and school, and that will give you one answer. For the other answers you need to imagine the problems it would cause within a large organisation. You could assume that there are some fairly major differences between the versions, if that makes the question easier to answer.

Suggested answer:

Documents created on the new version of the software will probably not be downwardly compatible so users in other departments will not be able to load and edit them.

Upgrading 'piecemeal' may cause difficulties with keeping track of site licences – the company may have a site licence to run a particular version of the software.

The computers in the department may not all be able to run the latest version of the software which probably will require more RAM, faster processor, more hard disk space etc. This may mean new hardware has to be purchased and could put an additional strain on the department budget. Current hardware may be leased and it would be expensive to terminate the lease early.

There is always movement between departments in a company and it is irritating and demotivating for, say, secretarial staff to find different versions of software when they move departments. Additional training may be required.

---

3. A hospital information system holds program files, which are rarely changed, and large database files, which are changing constantly. At present the backup strategy uses a tape storage device, and has the following characteristics:

Each evening the information system is taken off-line and a full backup is made of the entire system. Three sets of tapes are in use and are referred to as sets A, B and C.

Set A is used one evening,

Set B is used the next evening,

Set C is used the following evening.

This sequence is then repeated, starting the next evening, with Set A again.

An advisor has suggested a change is required to improve this strategy. Give, with reasons, **four** changes that could be made. (8)

NEAB IT05 Qu 5 1999

Notes:

Read Chapter 53 on Security and Backup Policies. You could suggest incremental backups, RAID systems, having more frequent or less frequent backups. Where are the backups stored? Remember, you must justify each point you make to get the second mark.

Suggested answer:

It is not necessary to backup the entire system every day. The hospital could use incremental backups so that on Monday, the whole system is backed up, on Tuesday, only the files created or changed on Tuesday are backed up, on Wednesday, only the files created or changed on Wednesday are backed up, etc. *(Now give a reason.)* This will reduce the amount of time spent on making backups.

The backup tapes should be securely stored off-site to give further protection against physical disaster.

The strategy should include regular restoration of files from the backup tapes to ensure that the backup system is working correctly and that in the event of a disaster the restoration process goes smoothly.

The hospital could use a RAID system (Redundant Array of Inexpensive Drives) so that all transactions are written to two separate drives, and if one drive goes down, the data is stored safely on the other drive. No further data will be written until both are up and running again.

(Could also say, need a backup log to keep records of which tape is the current one, and to keep a record of any problems with backups. Could use data compression techniques to reduce the backup time and amount of space required on storage media.)

---

4. You are the IT manager of a college. Your principal wishes to implement a computerised student identification card system. One way of providing the software for this system is to use a generic applications package, and to customise it to meet the project specification.

   (a) Describe **two** ways of providing the software other than using a 'generic applications package'. (4)

   (b) The college has a clearly set out IT strategy, however this project has not been included. Identify and describe **four** issues that should be considered when making a final choice from the above three methods. (8)

NEAB IT05 Qu 5 1998

Notes:

A 'generic applications package' is something like a spreadsheet or database package which you can use to build your own application, in the same way as you are presumably doing for at least one of your projects. Look at Chapter 62 on Software Acquisition for other ways of acquiring software.

Suggested answer:

(a) The software could be written in-house using a programming language such as Visual Basic. This would require a team of experienced programmers employed by the college.

Alternatively, a specific purpose applications package could be purchased. The package would have to be carefully evaluated to ensure that it met the requirements of the proposed system.

(b) Four issues:

Development time: It would be a lengthy process to develop an application from scratch using a team of analysts/programmers. It would also be necessary to already have, or to employ, analysts/programmers with the necessary skills.

Reliability of the system: Special purpose packages have usually been tried and tested and are therefore on the whole robust and do not crash unexpectedly, as they have been tested in many similar environments.

Availability of user training: There is often an authorised training program and/or training manuals for a special purpose system, which there would not be for the other two options.

System documentation: Packages usually come with documentation already complete, whereas this would have to be written for a system developed in-house and is often a rather neglected part of a project.

(Could also mention upgradeability, software support issues, compatibility with existing hardware/software.)

---

5. A company makes use of a computerised flat file information storage and retrieval system. The company is experiencing problems due to the use of this flat file system.

(a) Describe **three** benefits that the company would gain by using a relational database as opposed to a flat file system.   *(6)*

(b) The company currently has three files in use; customer, stock and orders. During conversion to a relational database system these files would need to be normalised. Explain clearly what you understand by the term normalisation.   *(2)*

(c) Examples from the three files are shown below. Normalise these files explaining any assumptions or additions you make to the files.   *(5)*

CUSTOMER FILE

Surname	Forename	Street	Town	City	Post Code
Smith	James	11 The Avenue	Bemersley	Ruston	RS12 5VF
Penfold	Jayne	67 Bathpool Road	Outclough	Wignall	WG5 6TY

ORDERS FILE

Surname	Forename	Post Code	Order Date	Item Ordered	Quantity Bought	Price	Total Cost	Paid
Smith	James	RS12 5VF	6/5/98	Magic Duster	2	£10.99	£21.98	Yes
Penfold	Jayne	WG5 6TY	1/6/98	Banana Rack	1	£12.50	£12.50	No
Smith	James	RS12 5VF	12/5/98	Winsor Doormat	1	£29.95	£29.95	Yes
Smith	James	RS12 5VF	12/5/98	Easee Food Grater	1	£11.99	£11.99	Yes
Penfold	Jayne	WG5 6TY	1/6/98	Winsor Doormat	1	£29.95	£29.95	No

STOCK FILE

Item Name	Price	Quantity in Stock
Winsor Doormat	£29.95	11
Magic Duster	£10.99	34
Electric Potato Peeler	£39.00	0
Easee Food Grater	£11.99	9
Banana Rack	£12.50	1

NEAB IT02 Qu 10 1998

Notes:

This is a very technical question and unless you have studied and understood database theory you have no hope. The good news is that if you have, this is an easy 13 marks. Remember that a flat file system is a system of separate unrelated files. A normalised database should not have the same information held on different files, except for the common fields that relate the two tables.

To answer part (c) you could start by first drawing an entity-relationship diagram so that you can see clearly how the three entities CUSTOMER, ORDER and STOCK are related. Your diagram should look something like this:

i.e. One customer may have many orders, but an order can only belong to one customer.

An order may be for many stock items, and a stock item may appear on many different orders.

Now the problem here is that you cannot have a many-to-many relationship in a normalised database (read all about it in Chapter 56.) You need to introduce a fourth table, which could be called ORDER_LINE (representing one line in an order consisting of several items ordered). The crow's feet turn round and you end up with:

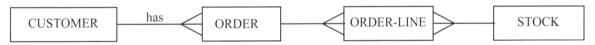

An order has many order lines.

An order-line is for one item of stock only, but a stock item may appear on several different order lines (in different orders).

Now you can create new tables from the original ones. Looking at the existing tables, none of them has a unique identifier which can act as the primary key, so you need to insert a primary key field in each table, e.g. CustID, OrderID, StockID. The new ORDER-LINE table needs 2 fields to make up the primary key – Order Number and either Line Number or Item Ordered.

The tables as they stand are already in First Normal Form because they contain no 'repeating fields', i.e. none of them have 2 fields for the same variable like Item Ordered.

The second step in normalisation is to make sure that each field in each table is dependent only on the primary key. This will get rid of the redundancy in the tables, so that for example Customer Name and Postcode is only held on the Customer file and not on the Orders file.

Once you've done all that, you'll probably have got the right answer. You could consider removing the Total Cost field from the Order table since this is a calculated field and it is not necessary to store it since it can be calculated when required.

Suggested answer:

(a) Advantages of relational database over a flat file system:

Data independence – the structure of the database does not affect programs which access it so for example an extra field could be added to the CUSTOMER table without needing to change programs not directly affected by the new field.

Control over redundancy (less data duplication. i.e. the same data is not stored several times on different files, so for example the video name and customer name are not stored on the LOAN table, as they can be looked up from the relevant table.

Consistency of data – because data is not duplicated there is no possibility of holding inconsistent data on different files, for example if a customer changes address.

(b) Normalisation is the process of organising data in related tables in such a way as to remove unnecessary redundancy (duplication of data), ensuring that there is consistency throughout the database. It also ensures that the database is flexible enough to enter as many or as few items (e.g. customer orders) as needed and to easily query the database.

(c) The normalised tables will look like this:

CUSTOMER FILE

CustID*	Surname	Forename	Street	Town	City	Post Code
123	Smith	James	11 The Avenue	Bemersley	Ruston	RS12 5VF
124	Penfold	Jayne	67 Bathpool Road	Outclough	Wignall	WG5 6TY

ORDERS FILE

OrderID*	Order Date	CustID	Paid
001	6/5/98	123	Yes
002	1/6/98	124	No
003	12/5/98	123	Yes

ORDER-LINE FILE

OrderID*	Item Ordered*	Quantity Bought
001	MD1	2
002	BR1	1
002	WD1	1
003	WD1	1
003	EFG1	1

STOCK FILE

StockID*	Item Name	Price	Quantity in Stock
WD1	Winsor Doormat	£29.95	11
MD1	Magic Duster	£10.99	34
EPP1	Electric Potato Peeler	£39.00	0
EFG1	Easee Food Grater	£11.99	9
BR1	Banana Rack	£12.50	1

* = Primary key

Total Cost field has been removed from the Order table since this is a calculated field and it is not necessary to store it since it can be calculated when required. Primary keys have been added.

6. A computer has a computer network system.

    (a) Activity on the network system is monitored and an accounting log is automatically produced.

        (i)   State **four** items of information that this log might include. (4)

        (ii) Give **four** reasons why such a log is useful. (4)

    (b) An IT consultant has suggested that the company changes from a peer-to-peer network to a server based network. Give **six** features of these network environments which contrast the two different approaches. (6)

    NEAB IT05 Qu 6 1999

Notes:

There are several reasons why a systems administrator might want to monitor activity on a network. Why do you think he/she might want to know who is using a network, for how long and what they are doing or looking at?

Suggested answer:

(a) (i)   Four items:

            Amount of time logged on for each user, and times of day logged on;

            Workstation from which each user logged on each time;

            Number of times network crashed and details of any error messages;

            Density of network traffic at each hour of day/night.

            (Could also say, details of files stored/updated/deleted, details of applications used/count of users per application, details of failed login attempts.)

    (ii) The log is useful because it provides systems administrators with information about network load so that they can deal with performance problems, or make informed decisions about whether to upgrade the network. It also helps to identify any abuse of the system or hackers trying to log on, e.g. if someone has 500 attempts to find the correct password. It helps to identify the busiest times of day so that rescheduling of some activities could possibly be done.

(b)   In a server based network:

There is no one machine controlling the network;

Shared software and data are stored on the server, on a peer-to-peer software is stored on individual machines;

Peer-to-peer is more suitable for linking a small number of computers where each user performs basically different tasks but sometimes needs to use data held on other computers in the network;

Software upgrades are easier to manage on a server based network since only one copy of the software is stored;

Security issues are harder to control on a peer-to-peer network;

The speed of access will vary with the number of users logged on in a server based network;

Backup is centrally managed on a server based network.

---

7. A supermarket chain has recently implemented a new stock control system in each of its branches. This has affected those staff who have not used computer systems before. Many of the staff have described the system as being 'user-friendly'. However, when the package was implemented in one particular store, it was not well received by its staff.

    (a) Give **four** features of software packages, that would merit the description *'user-friendly'*. (4)

    (c) Both physical and psychological factors can influence how people interact with computer systems. Both may have contributed to the poor reception of this system in that store.

(i)   Describe **two** such physical factors.

(ii) Describe **two** such psychological factors.   (8)

NEAB IT05 Qu 7 1999

Notes:

This should be easy enough. I've no advice to give!

Suggested answer:

(a) User friendly: Intuitive to use; context-sensitive help available; commands, menus etc. in familiar places on screen, with a similar menu structure to other packages. Wizards or short cuts available to perform common tasks. Effective use of sound/colour to assist users.

(b) (i)   Physical factors: could be placed in a noisy environment so that sound effects associated with tasks cannot be heard; could be badly positioned so that the screen is not easily read with glare or reflection; the choice of colour scheme could be poor.

(ii) Psychological factors: the system could have been introduced with no training or preparation and people could be biased against it; the users in this particular store may be older people who are afraid of computers or who have been using the old system for the past 30 years and don't want to waste all that expertise.

---

8. A software company is preparing to release a new application program. Describe the two types of testing carried out before the final release of the software. Explain why both are needed.   (6)

NEAB IT05 Qu 5 1997

Notes:

The expected answer to this question is exactly what is in the specification (what used to be known as the syllabus) – alpha and beta testing. To do well in this exam you are strongly advised to become very familiar with the specification, which you will find in the back of this book. Use it as a basis for your revision.

Suggested answer:

Alpha testing (also known as acceptance testing). This is the final stage in the testing process before the system is accepted for operational use. It involves testing the system with data provided by the software house. It will continue until there is agreement among the design/development team that the system fulfils all the requirements of the specification.

Beta testing. This involves giving the package to a number of potential users who agree to use the system and report any problems to the developers. Microsoft, for example, delivers beta versions of their products to hundreds of sites for testing. This exposes the product to real use and detects problems and errors that may not have been anticipated by the developers. The product can then be modified and sent out for further beta testing until the developer is confident enough in the product to put it on the market.

Both types of testing are needed because in-house testing will reveal errors or omissions both in the systems requirement definition and in the system developed. These must be fixed before the application is given to outside users to test. The beta testing is useful because it exposes the software to a large number of users who may use it in unexpected ways, and it will be tried on machines with different specifications using real data. This is likely to result in errors or omissions coming to light, or to highlight improvements that need to be made before the software can be put on general release.

---

9. "The rise of de facto standards due to commercial sales success can only benefit organisations and individuals". Discuss this statement.

   Particular attention should be given to:

   - operating systems;
   - portability of data between applications;
   - portability of data between different computer systems.

   Illustrate your answer with specific examples. (16)

   Quality of language will be assessed in this answer.

   NEAB IT02 Qu 11 1999

Notes:

Look at the advice given for question 9 at the end of IT01 on writing essays. You need to make four hard-hitting points and discuss them for each part of the question. A further 4 marks are available for a general discussion of issues if you have not managed to reach 12 yet, but don't just keep wittering on and on in case in the end you say something worth a mark. The final 4 marks will be for quality of language and coherence of answer and you'll lose marks here if you don't stick to the point.

Suggested answer:

Windows has become a de facto standard for PC operating systems around the world. This has the benefit that whatever PC you buy, Windows will almost certainly be pre-installed and will be familiar to someone who has previously used a PC. It should also mean that because of the gigantic volume of sales it is extremely cheap but this is not in fact the case. Some critics would also say that Microsoft has done the world a disservice by stifling the creative efforts of developers who from time to time come up with much better operating systems, but cannot break the virtual monopoly enjoyed by Microsoft by virtue of its world dominance.

The strict control exerted by Microsoft over its operating system has, however, meant that only one version of, say, Windows 98 or Windows 2000 exists. This is in contrast to Unix, say, which has been develop and 'improved' by many companies, leading to hardware and software compatibility problems.

The virtual monopoly enjoyed by Microsoft with its Windows operating system may be challenged by a newer operating system called Linux, which is available free on the Internet. Some of the best programmers in the world have worked on it, and it may yet establish itself as a de facto standard. It is less 'buggy' than Windows and more efficient in terms of memory space. Many of Microsoft's competitors – IBM, Corel and Borland, are beginning to offer Linux versions of their software. This will be of great benefit to everyone because it is free – Windows 2000 costs around £260.

The portability of data between applications means that, for example, graphics created in Corel Draw or a pie chart created in Excel can be imported into Word. Objects can also be linked into another application such as a Word document, in such a way that when the spreadsheet or graphic is edited, the latest version will appear automatically in the Word document.

The ASCII standard is an example of a de facto standard for representing characters. It is used on all personal computers and enables the transfer of text data between applications and between different computer systems. On the Internet, the adoption of the TCP/IP protocol as a de facto standard has meant that it is possible to download information from computers all over the world. This has led to a huge increase in the number of people accessing the World Wide Web and is clearly an enormous benefit to all. Communications protocols such as the OSI standard protocol means that data can be transferred between different computer systems on a local or wide area network. The protocol lays down exactly what format the data has to be in and how it is to be transmitted.

Programs written in the language Java will run on any hardware platform – a great benefit to Web page designers and users as it is widely used in interactive Web page design.

Appendix A

AQA Specification Summary

Information and Communications Technology

Scheme of Assessment – Advanced Level (AS+A2)

The Scheme of Assessment has a modular structure. The A Level award comprises three compulsory assessment units from the AS Scheme of Assessment and three compulsory assessment units from the A2 scheme of assessment.

AS Assessment Units

Unit 1	Written Paper	1 ½ hours

15% of the total A Level marks

Short answer and structured questions.

Unit 2	Written Paper	1 ½ hours

15% of the total A Level marks

Short answer and structured questions.

Unit 3	Coursework	

20% of the total A Level marks — *60 marks*

A2 Assessment Units

Unit 4	Written Paper	2 hours

15% of the total A Level marks

Short answer, structured questions and an essay.

Unit 5	Written Paper	2 hours

15% of the total A Level marks

Short answer, structured questions and an essay.

Unit 6	Coursework	

20% of the total A Level marks — *90 marks*

A2 Module 4 – Information Systems within Organisations

	Topic	Amplification	See Chapter
4.1	**Organisational structure**	Understand the basic concepts of organisational structure as they impact on/affect ICT systems.	36
4.2	**Information systems and organisations**	Understand the difference between an information system and a data processing system. Understand the role and relevance of an information system in aiding decision making.	36
	Definition of a Management Information System	Recall that an MIS is a system to convert data from internal and external sources into information. This is communicated in an appropriate form to managers at different levels to enable them to make effective decisions for planning, directing and controlling the activities for which they are responsible.	37
	The development and life cycle of an information system	Recognise the existence of formal methods, the need for clear time scales, deliverables and approval to proceed.	38
	Success or failure of a Management Information System	Understand the factors influencing the success or failure of an information system: inadequate analysis, lack of management involvement in design, emphasis on computer system, concentration on low-level data processing, lack of management knowledge of ICT systems and their capabilities, inappropriate/excessive management demands, lack of teamwork, lack of professional standards.	39
4.3	**Corporate information systems strategy**	Describe the factors influencing an information system within an organisation: management organisation and functions, planning and decision making methods, legal and audit requirement, general organisation structure, responsibility for the information system within an organisation, information flow, hardware and software, standard, behavioural factors e.g. personalities, motivation, ability to adapt to change.	40
	Information flow	Describe the methods and mechanisms of information flow within an organisation both formal and informal and the constraints imposed upon this by organisational structures.	42
	Personnel	Understand the levels of task/personnel within an organisation: strategic, implementation, operational and relate the needs of these three levels to the information system.	36

	Topic	Amplification	See Chapter
4.4	**Information and Data**		
	Information	Understand management information needs; the concept of relevance and methods of interpretation.	42
		Understand that information has many characteristics and can be classified in many ways. Examples include:	
		Source - internal, external, primary, secondary; Nature - quantitative, qualitative, formal, informal; Level - strategic, tactical, operational; Time - historical, current, future; Frequency - real-time, hourly, daily, monthly; Use - planning, control, decision; Form - written, visual, aural, sensory; Type - disaggregated, aggregated sampled;	
		Discuss the value of information in aiding the decision making process.	
		Understand the difference between internal and external information requirements.	
		Describe the characteristics of good information and delivery: relevant, accurate, complete, user confidence, to right person, at right time, in right detail, via correct channel of communication, understandable.	
		Describe the advantages and characteristics of good information within an applications context.	
	Effective Presentation	Understand the effect that the method and style of presentation has upon the message – design in relation to the intended audience.	42
	Data	Understand that data may require translation or transcription prior to entry into the system. This can affect the accuracy of the data.	43
		Discuss the impact of quantity and quality of data on the method of data capture and the control and audit mechanisms required to manage the data capture.	
4.5	**The management of change**	Understand that the introduction or development of an information system will result in change which must be managed. Changes could occur in relation to re-skilling, attitude, organisational structure, employment pattern and conditions, internal procedures.	44
4.6	**Legal aspects**	Understand the need for a corporate information system security policy and the role it would fill within an organisation. Factors could include prevention of misuse, detection, investigation, procedures, staff responsibilities, disciplinary procedures.	45
		Describe the content of a corporate information technology security policy.	46
		Describe methods of improving awareness of security policy within an organisation, cross referencing to training and standards.	47

	Topic	Amplification	See Chapter
	Audit requirements	Understand that many information systems are subject to audit. Understand the impact of audit on data and information control. Describe the need for audit and the role of audit management/software tools in information systems. Understand the function of audit trails and describe applications of their use; e.g. ordering systems, student tracking, police vehicle enquiries.	45
	Disaster recovery management	Describe the various potential threats to information systems. Factors could include; physical security, document security, personnel security, hardware security, communications security, software security. Understand the concept of risk analysis. Understand the commercial need to ensure that an information system is protected from threat. Describe a range of contingency plans to recover from disasters and relate these to identified threats. Describe the criteria used to select a contingency plan appropriate to the scale of an organisation and installation.	46
	Legislation	Understand that the implementation of legislation will impact on the procedures within an organisation. Describe the methods of enforcing and controlling data protection legislation within an organisation. Describe the methods of enforcing and controlling software misuse legislation within an organisation. Describe the methods of enforcing and controlling health and safety legislation within an organisation. Discuss the implications of the various types of legislation.	47
4.7	**User Support**	Describe the ways in which software houses provide user support; relate these to cost and package credibility. Describe the range of user support options available when using industry standard packages. These could include: existing user base, support articles, utilities, specialist bulletin boards, communications systems eg Internet, e-mail. Select and justify an appropriate user support system for a particular context. Explain the need for different levels of documentation related to user and task.	48

	Topic	Amplification	See Chapter
	Training	Explain the need for different levels of training related to user and task.	49
		Understand the need for continual skill updating and refreshing.	
		Describe the methods by which users can gain expertise in software use and discuss their relative merits.	
		Understand the need to develop training strategies to respond to growing user awareness.	
4.8	**Project management and effective ICT teams**	Understand why projects are often sub-divided into tasks and allocated to teams.	50
		Describe the characteristics of a good team; leadership, appropriate allocation of tasks, adherence to standards, monitoring, costing, controlling.	
4.9	**Information and the professional**	Discuss the social, moral and ethical issues associated with the introduction and use of information and communication technology systems as they affect a professional working within the industry.	51
		Understand that 'codes of practice' exist separate from any legal requirements with which professional organisations are expected to comply.	
		Understand the need for a code of practice for ICT users in an organisation.	
	Employee Code of Conduct	Understand what is meant by an employee code of conduct; e.g. responsibilities, authorisation, security, penalties for misuse.	51
		Describe the contents of such a code of conduct.	

A2 Module 5 – Information: Policy, Strategy and Systems

	Topic	Amplification	See Chapter
5.1	**Policy and strategy issues**	Understand the need for an information technology policy.	52
		Understand the strategic implications of software, hardware and configuration choices for an organisation.	
		Appreciate the range of needs of different users.	
	Methods of enhancing existing capabilities – Future proofing	Discuss the reasons why organisations may wish to upgrade hardware/software provision - factors could include hardware/software development, organisation ethos, task driven change, software change.	52
		Understand that hardware and software exists which allows packages to run on different platforms, and the advantages and disadvantages of the approach.	
	Backup strategies	Describe the different options available for backup systems and understand the implications and limitations of their use.	53
		Understand the strategies for backup scheduling and storage of backups.	
5.2	**Software**		
	Evaluation of software	Describe the mechanisms/procedures for software evaluation e.g. establish client/user needs, establish software capabilities and match.	54
	Evaluation criteria	Understand the need for establishing evaluation criteria; these include	54

		Agreed problem specification
		Functionality
		Performance – use of benchmarks
		Usability and human-machine interfaces
		Compatibility with existing software base
		Transferability of data
		Robustness
		User support
		Resource requirements including hardware, software and human
		Upgradability
		Portability
		Financial issues –
		   development cost
		   development opportunities	

	Topic	Amplification	See Chapter

	Evaluation report	Understand the function of an evaluation report and know that the content will include:
		   methodology used
		   actual evaluation
		   recommendations
		   justification.
			54

5.3	**Database management concepts**	Explain the purpose of a database management system (DBMS). Explain the role of the database administrator. Explain what is meant by data consistency, data integrity, data redundancy and data independence. Explain the concept of entity relationships and data normalisation.	55,57 57 56
5.4	**Communication and information systems** **Applications of communication and information systems** **Distributed systems** **Client/server systems**	Describe the use of networked systems for various applications. Describe the network infrastructure required to support the World Wide Web. Select and justify an appropriate networked system for a particular application. Understand that distribution can apply to both data and control. Describe the uses of distributed databases and understand the advantages and limitations of such distribution. Describe the concept of a client/server database. Recall the relevant advantages of a client/server database over a non-client/server database.	58 58 58 57 57
5.5	**Networks** **Network security, audit and accounting**	Understand the particular security, audit and accounting problems associated with networks, and recall the steps which can be taken to preserve security. Describe the measures taken to protect network traffic against illegal access. Understand the reasons for using audit software in providing a network service. Understand the reasons for using accounting software in providing a network service.	59

	Topic	Amplification	See Chapter
	Network environments	Understand how a network environment affects the user interface provided: security, control of software, control of files - access rights.	59
5.6	**Human/ Computer Interaction**	Describe the psychological factors that affect human/computer interaction; user friendly, give help to novices, provide short cuts for experts, make use of human long term memory to maximise efficiency.	61
5.7	**Human/ Computer Interface**	Recall different approaches to the problem of communication with ICT systems and discuss the resource implications of sophisticated HCI. Discuss the implications for customising software to develop a specialist HCI.	61
5.8	**Software development**	Understand that there are different ways of providing software solutions to specialist applications: - user written, internal development team/department - external software house to specification. Describe the possible criteria for selection of software solutions to specialist applications and their place within the corporate strategy.	62
5.9	**Software reliability**	Describe methods of ensuring that software is reliable: α testing, β testing, agreements between software houses and purchaser for testing. Understand the reasons why fully-tested software may fail to operate successfully when implemented as part of an information technology system. Understand the need for maintenance release(s).	62
5.10	**Portability of data**		
	Protocols and standards	Explain the need for portability of data, ease of transferring numerical, graphical and textual data between applications. Describe the need for standards for interchanging numerical, graphical and textual data between different hardware and software platforms.	60
	Communication standards	Know of the existence, benefits and limitations of standards. Understand the protocols and addressing mechanisms used to support the World Wide Web.	60
	Emergence of standards	Recognise the existence of de facto standards based on historic precedent and sales success in comparison to formal standards.	60

Index

1NF...305
2NF...307
3NF...307
Access
   control...323
   privileges..323
Alpha testing...339
Attribute...302
Audit
   controls...324
   trail...249
Authorisation software..............................248
Backup
   full...292
   hardware...293
   incremental...292
   on-line..294
   strategy...291
Bar code...237
Baseband...327
Benchmark tests..298
Beta testing..339
British Computer Society..........................272
Broadband...327
Bulletin boards...262
Business Software Alliance.......................256
Call centres..262
Centralised processing system.................314
Change management....................................241
Changeover................................See Conversion
Channels of communication......................232
Client-server..315
   database..312
Code of conduct...............................272, 274
Code of Ethics...272
Codes of practice..274
Communications
   software..327
Compatible hardware and software.........288
Computer-based training...........................266
Conceptual data model..............................301
Conversion
   direct/parallel/phased/pilot...................214
Copyright Designs and Patents Act.........256
Corporate training strategy......................267
Critical success factor...............................286
Data
   consistency...300
   dictionary...310
   encryption..325
   processing systems....................................200

Protection Act...255
   redundancy...300
   shareable...300
Database..300
   administrator..310
   client-server...312
   distributed..317
   Management System..........................301, 311
   relational..304
DBA..310
DBMS..301, 311
De facto standards...............................328, 329
De jure standards.......................................328
Decision
   making..205
   management..205
   structured...205
   unstructured...205
Disaster
   planning..252
   recovery plan...253
Dispersed system..314
Distributed
   database..317
   processing...316
Documentation..264
Domain
   Name System...330
   top-level...330
EDI..237
Electronic
   data interchange.......................................237
Employee code of conduct.........See Code of conduct
Emulation software.....................................288
Encryption...325
End-user computing....................................225
Entity..302
Entity-relationship diagram.....................302
Ethics..272
Evaluation report.......................................298
Exception report...230
Expert system...228
Failure, of information systems...............241
Feasibility study...212
Firewall..324
First normal form.......................................305
Flat-file..308
Foreign key..304
Future proofing...289
Gateway..321
Golden Rule...274

Grandfather-father-son 294
Greatest Good/Least Harm 274
Handshaking 248
Health and Safety..258
Help desk 260
http..330
Human-computer interaction 332
Implementation....................................214, 218, 221
Incompatible hardware and software....................288
Information
    external 202, 230
    flow...203
    internal...202, 230
    levels of 230
    management..286
    operational 230
    presenting 232
    quality of..230
    sources 230
    strategic..230
    tactical..230
Information system 200
    management...202
    operational 202
    strategy 224
Integrity of data 246
Internet..320
    backbone 320
    protocol...329
    Service Provider 321, 330
ISP 321
Kant's Categorical Imperative 274
Knowledge
    -based system..228
    work system 201
LAN...315
Legacy system 289
Levels in an organisation 200
Long-term memory..333
Magnetic
    stripe 237
Maintenance
    adaptive...215
    corrective 215
    perfective 215
Maintenance release 340
Management information system 201
    desirable characteristics 207
    failure of 207, 241
Many-to-Many relationship 307
Methods of conversion 214
Microsoft 329
MIS ....*See* Management Information System
Modem..327
Network
    public 320

Network service providers....................................320
Newsletters 263
Normalisation 305
NSP..320
On-line
    help 263
Open System Interface...328
Operational information 230
Operational level 200
Organisational levels 200
Organisations...196
Parallel conversion 214
Partial dependency...307
Peer-to-peer 315
Performance management 324
Personnel safeguards 250
Phased conversion 214
Pilot conversion 214
Platform 288
Post-implementation review 215
Presentation 234
Professional
    conduct 272
Program-data dependence....................................300
Project
    manager 269
    planning 270
    reviews..271
    team 269
Protocol 328
    ftp...330
    http..330
    TCP/IP...329
Prototyping 216
Proxy server...324
Public network 320
Query by example...311
RAID 294
Relation 304
Relational database 304
Relationship...302
Requirements analysis 213
Risk analysis 246
Router 321, 324
Second normal form 307
Security..323
    of data 246
    plan 253
    policy 250
Server...315, 321
Short-term memory..333
Slippery Slope Rule 274
Smart card..238
Software
    acquisition...336
    copyright...256

designing good 334
evaluation 297
leasing...337
maintenance..340
selecting..338
tailoring..297
testing 338
testing, failure of..339
upgradability..297
SQL 312
Stakeholder...199
Strategic information 230
Strategic level 200
Structured Query Language............................312
Support articles 263
SWOT analysis 223
System
data processing 200
design..214
failure..241
information 200
knowledge work 201
maintenance..215
transaction processing................................200
Systems life cycle 210
Tactical information 230

Tactical level 200
TCP/IP..329
Technical support 260
Testing..338
Third normal form 307, 308
Top level domain 330
Training 265
Transaction
processing system.......................................200
Transmission
asynchronous...328
parallel...328
serial..328
speed..327
synchronous..328
Uniform Resource Locator 330
Upgradability..297
Upgrading 289
URL...330
User
booklets 263
WAN 316
Waterfall model 211
Web
address...330
World Wide Web...320